How It Came to Be

The Boyd Family's Contribution

to

African American Religious Publishing

from the 19th to the 21st Century

Bobby L. Lovett

Printed by Lightning Source Press
Lavergne, Tennessee

HOW IT CAME TO BE by Bobby L. Lovett
Copyright © 2007 by Mega Publishing Corporation, Nashville, TN

ISBN 1-890436-27-5

Printed in the United States of America

Lovett, Bobby L.
How It Came To Be

Photographs and Illustrations

Chapter One

First Staff for the NBPB, 1896
Book Bindery
M & G Group in Texas
Rev. William Marion
Margaret V. McKicken
Meharry Dental & Pharm. Hall
Meharry Medical College
Meharry Nurses
Monuments of R.H. Boyd

Chapter Two

Rev. Charles Henry Clark
Rev. J. P. Robinson
Boyd Family, 1890s
NBPB Chorus, Early 1900s

Chapter Three

Baptist Ministers Alliance
Mrs. L.P. Benham
Old NBPB Plant and Headquarters, 1910
Dr. C.J.W. Boyd
H.A. Boyd Band
Mrs. H.A. Boyd
Mrs. R.H. Boyd
R.H. Boyd
R.H. Boyd Memorial Building
R.H. Thorburne "Our Missionary in Panama"
Bessie Thorburne, NBPB's Missionary to Panama
R.H. Boyd, President
H.A. Boyd and R.H. Boyd
Rev. S.N. Vass
Col. W.S. Bradden, D.D.
Rev. W.W. Brown
Miss N.H. Burroughs
Rev. E.C. Morris
Rev. H. J. Moses
Mt. Olive B.C. Usher Board
Mrs. Jenie B. Paul Murphy
National Baptist Revised Hymnal
National Jubilee Melodies

National Baptist Banner
Founders and Directors of One Cent Savings Bank and Trust
        Company, Nashville, 1904

Chapter Four

James C. Napier, Manager of One Cent Savings Bank
J. W. Bostic
Chicago Ministers & Deacons Alliance
Church Record Roll and Minute Book
Citizens Savings Bank President's Dinner
Citizens Savings Bank President's Dinner
Citizens Bank & Trust Co.
Mrs. O. W. Coleman
Congress Secretaries & Officials Parade
Congress Band
Congress Entertainment Committee

Chapter Five

Henry Allen Boyd, Secretary-Treasurer, NBPB, 1922-1959
Wedding of Georgia Bradford and Henry Allen Boyd, 1908
Henry Allen Boyd and Associates Prepare for Trip
National Baptist Publishing Board Plant, Nashville, 1920s
NBPB Headquarters, Nashville, 1950s
F. Benjamin Davis, Th.D.
Ebenezer Baptist Church
Ebenezer Groundbreaking
Ebenezer Baptist Sunday School Band
        Golden Gems Book
Grads E.H. Branch and Dr. C. Clay
1930 Convention, Chicago
Henry Allen Boyd Band
H.A. Boyd, T.B. Boyd Jr., Sims & Eppse
Negro Doll Ad
Meharry Brass Band
National Escorts Congress: Dallas
Rev. G. L. Prince
Rev. J. B. Ridley
Rev. Henry Allen Boyd
Ms. Sadie B. Wilson
Sunday School Literature

Chapter Six

Dr. T.B. Boyd, Jr., Secretary-Treasurer, NBPB (NBR)
T.B. Boyd, Jr.

Mrs. T.B. Boyd, Jr. (Mable Landrum)
NBPB Publication for Children (T.B. Boyd, Jr.'s children)
NBPB Employees working in Old Plant
NBPB Employees in the Old Plant (T.B. Boyd, Sr. at far left,
    back row)
T.B. Boyd, Jr. visits Church Ewing and Oscar Crawford at
    New Print Machines
Gilbert King adjusts a printing press at Old NBPB
T.B. Boyd Jr., Ch. Leaders Talk
Employees Adjust Machines at Publishing House, Nashville
Dr. Richard H. Dixon, Sr. with President Lyndon Johnson
Rev. J. Royster Powell
T.B. Boyd Jr. and Dr. Dixon with Statue
Dr. M.L. King with T.B. Boyd Jr. in Chicago
N.Y. Pro. Bap. Con. Leaders

Chapter Seven
Dr. T.B. Boyd III, President & CEO of R.H. Boyd Publishing
    Corporation
Rev. W.N. Daniel and Antioch Baptist Church, Chicago
Dr. S.M. Lockridge
Dr. Nehemiah Davis
Dr. S.M. Wright and Family
National Missionary Baptist Convention of America Officers

Chapter Eight
Dr. F. Benjamin Davis, Chairman National Baptist Publishing
    Board
The NBPB Sunday School Congress, 1988
Rev. Jim Holley, Ph.D.
Dr. Gregory Moss
Cadets and Dancers in Congress Parade, 2002

Epilogue
Boyd Christmas, 2003
The R.H. Boyd Publishing Corporation, 6717 Centennial
    Boulevard, Nashville, TN
National Missionary Baptist Convention of America, 1988
Yvette Boyd
First Class Mailing Department
The NBPB and NMBCA Sunday School Congress
Company Brochures

All photographs are courtesy of the NBPB/R.H. Boyd Corporation

Contents

Photographs and Illustrations

Foreword ix

Acknowledgments xi

Preface xvii

Chapter 1
Genesis: The Early Life & Times of Richard Henry Boyd, 1843-1895 1

Chapter 2
1896-1905: Early Years of the National Baptist Publishing Board 27

Chapter 3
1906-1922: Maturity, Controversy, Growth, and the End of an Era for the
Publishing Board 53

Chapter 4
R.H. Boyd: Entrepreneur, Business Manager, and Leader 77

Chapter 5
1922-1959: Henry Allen Boyd, 37 Years at the Helm of the NBPB 85

Chapter 6
1959-1979: T.B. Boyd, Jr. and the New Era
of the Publishing Business 109

Chapter 7
1979-1996: T.B. Boyd III Takes the NBPB to the End of the
First 100 Years 125

Chapter 8
1996–Present: T.B. Boyd III and Transformations of the National Baptist
Publishing Board and R.H. Boyd Publishing Corporation 155

Epilogue 175

Appendixes 193

Selected Bibliography 203

Index 207

Foreword

I have been pleased to receive and examine *"How It Came To Be: The Boyd Family's Contribution to African American Publishing from the 19th Century to the 21st Century."*

The saga in this family's record is contained in the title of the book. One will look long, and likely in vain, to find an American family with four generations of distinguished service. Add to that the incredible fact that this bright procession began with Richard Henry Boyd who experienced the horrors of chattel slavery and it becomes unmistakably clear that here we have the material of which sheer heroism is made.

Astonishment grows at contemplation of an unbroken succession which amounts to nothing less than a publishing dynasty, originating among a people who by law, de Jure, were not allowed to learn to read.

Four generations of publishers, continuing now brilliantly in T.B. Boyd III, provide incontrovertible conclusion that with faith in God "all things are possible." The moral of this inspiring chronicle: creativity creates controversy, creativity almost always conquers. Ad astra per Aspera

Gardner Taylor, D.D.
Pastor Emeritus
The Concord Baptist Church of Christ

Acknowledgments

Several writers have published books about black Baptists and have included stories about the National Baptist Publishing Board. The first published history of the National Baptist Publishing Board was *A Story of the National Baptist Publishing Board* (1915) by Richard H. Boyd. In 1924, after the Reverend Boyd's death, a second edition of *A Story of the National Baptist Publishing Board* was subtitled *The Why, How, When, Where, and By Whom It Was Established.* The Reverend Charles Henry Clark, chairman of the board of directors for the NBPB, and other board members wrote an appendix for the 1924 edition. Henry Allen Boyd directed the compilation of that edition, a 155 page pocket-size book.

As early as 1911, the National Baptist Publishing Board (NBPB) produced Nathaniel A. Pius' *Outline of Baptist History* as a tool to teach Sunday school students and other Negro Baptists the background of the Baptist faith. Lewis G. Jordan published *The History of Black Baptists* (1936) through the National Baptist Convention, USA, Inc. Jordan's account used as much objectivity as possible to describe the struggle to organize a national convention and discuss the denominational split of 1915, and other studies subsequently have followed. Owen D. Pelt and Ralph L. Smith published *The Story of the National Baptists* (1961), which offers valuable information about the origins and progress of the National Baptist Convention, USA, Inc. Leroy Fitts attempted an objective account of the denominational splits among the Negro Baptists, titled *A History of Black Baptists* (1985). According to William H. Brackney, *The Baptists* (1988), some recent denominational histories have improved with greater reliance on primary sources and more rigorous scholastic standards. There is still more work to be done, especially in defining a story on the precise beginnings of the Negro Baptist church to include the Silver Bluff Baptist Church in South Carolina and the First African Baptist Church in Savannah, Georgia.

This newest book about the Boyd family and their religious publishing ventures explores historical sources through newspapers, books, journals, biographies, personal papers, official records, census data, city directories, photographs, tax records, court records, and microfilm documents. These sources may be accessed at the Southern Baptist Convention's Historical Commission, National Archives and Records Service, National Baptist Publishing Board, the Tennessee State Library and Archives, Tennessee State University Library's Special Collections, Nashville Public Library's Nashville Room collection, and Fisk University Library's Special Collection. Papers previously belonging to James Marion Frost were reviewed at the SBC's archives. I also investigated and recorded the following organizations' journals and minutes: National Baptist Convention, 1895-1915; National Baptist Convention of America (Unincorporated), 1916-1988; National Missionary Baptist Convention of America, 1988-1991; National Baptist Convention of the United States of America (Incorporated), 1916-1922; Journal of the Northern Baptist Convention, 1908-1916; Annual Report of the Southern Baptist Convention, 1890-1981; Annual Reports of the National Baptist Publishing Board; Annual Reports of the American Baptist Publication Society; Annual Reports of the American Baptist Home Mission Society.

I reviewed and noted the annual reports for the National Baptist Convention's Foreign Mission Board, the Women's Auxiliary Board, the Home Mission Board, the Baptist Young People's Union Board, the Sunday School Congress, and the Baptist Training Union. The Southern Baptist Convention's Historical Commission housed hard copies of the journal for the Southern Baptist Convention and the Northern Baptist Convention. Some microfilm copies of the journals for the National Baptist Convention and other conventions also were available at the Historical Commission.

Particularly during the tenure of T.B. Boyd III, the NBPB preserved many hard copies of the National Baptist Convention's journals, as well as convention programs and publications for the Sunday School Congress. Many issues of the *National Baptist Union*,

National Baptist Review, and the subsequent *National Baptist Union-Review* existed on microfilm at the Southern Baptist Convention's Historical Commission and other libraries. T.B. Boyd III and the NBPB had laminated and preserved extensive volumes of original pages of the *National Baptist Union,* the *National Baptist Union-Review,* and the *Nashville Globe.* The NBPB, whose archives are well organized and exceptionally secured, also made available hard copies of most recent issues of the *National Baptist Union-Review,* the Sunday School Congress program booklets, and denominational convention journals. The Tennessee State Library and Archives (TSLA) furnished many microfilm copies of the *National Baptist Voice,* the official periodical of the National Baptist Convention, USA. The TSLA microfilmed newspaper files and the archives division are invaluable to any historian doing research on Tennessee history.

All photographs were furnished through the courtesy of the Publishing Board, the R.H. Boyd Publishing Corporation, its publications, or from the pages of the *Nashville Globe.* The late Mrs. Mable L. Boyd—an exemplary woman who loved her husband and kept the memory of him until the day of her death—provided me with a brief interview on her life, some information about her husband, T.B. Boyd, Jr., and some personal photographs. Otherwise, I did not rely on interviews for fear of tainting the story. Not even T.B. Boyd III was interviewed at length for this story. My technique was to ask questions and conduct interviews when and if the story had confusing and complex points that perhaps a living person could clarify, or when written historical documentation may not be available at the time of researching and writing the narrative.

This proved to be an extensive research project for me; and since the last book, I have been able to clarify and broaden parts of the story after listening to comments and NBPB stories from others. I also found helpful the works of many other writers who helped place events in proper perspective through their books: Gayraud S. Wilmore, *Black Religion and Black Radicalism: An Interpretation of the Religious History of Afro-American People* (1973); James M. Washington, *Frustrated Fellowship: The Black Baptist Quest for Social Power* (1986); William D. Booth, *The Progressive Story: New Baptist Roots* (1981); Carter G. Woodson, *The History of the Negro Church* (1921); Joseph H. Jackson, *A Story of Activism: The History of the*

National Baptist Convention, U.S.A. (1980); E. Franklin Frazier, *The Negro Church in America* (1963); Leroy Fitts, *Lott Carey: First Black Missionary to Africa* (1979); and Edward A. Freeman, *The Epoch of Negro Baptists and the Foreign Mission Board* (1953). These and other publications helped me to understand the black Baptist saga, which is difficult to interpret. Books by William E.B. DuBois, *The Negro in the South: His Economic Progress in Relation to His Moral and Religious Development* (1907) and Walter B. Weare, *Black Business in the New South: A Social History of the North Carolina Mutual Insurance Company* (1973), served as exemplary models of early black business histories.

Rather than rely on hearsay, legends, rumors, and personal recollections, I researched wills, deeds, census data, court records, and city directories at the Tennessee State Library and Archives (TSLA) in Nashville. I also used printed and microfilm census data regarding Texas. For general census data, I relied on the Census Bureau's website, which has state and county data from historical periods. I gained access to some books, bibliographies, and city directories at the Nashville Public Library, whose staff in the Nashville Room has always kindly treated me and promptly acted in meeting my requests. All these public records proved valuable in the process of corroborating evidence and personal recollections, myths, legends, and factual data. Computer, Internet, and other electronic searches were utilized to locate additional information, including archives and libraries across the nation such as the Schomburg Collection at the Harlem branch of the New York Public Library. I also used the J.C. Napier (1845-1940) Papers at Fisk University's library.

The president and chief executive officer, Theophilus Bartholomew Boyd III, as well as the board members and officers of the NBPB and R.H. Boyd Publishing Corporation are appreciated for remaining conscious of historical preservation of institutional documents and for their cooperation and support of researchers who visited headquarters and utilized their assistance. Again, the preservation and organization of certain publications, documents, and photographs is commendable on their part and a valuable service to the maintenance of American history. Without this service, the details herein would be less complete.

— Bobby L. Lovett (August 17, 2006)

Preface

The Reverend Richard Henry Boyd, who was born a slave in 1843, became an entrepreneur, banker, businessman, philanthropist, and religious and civic leader. Besides founding the National Baptist Publishing Board, he helped organize the Nashville chapter of the National Negro Business League (1902), One Cent Savings and Trust Company Bank (1904), National Negro Doll Company (1905), Union Transportation Streetcar Company (1906), Globe Newspaper Publishing Company (1906), National Baptist Church Furniture Manufacturing Company (1908), Nashville Negro Board of Trade (1912), Nashville Colored Young Men's Christian Association (1917), and a Baptist seminary in Nashville (1918). Richard Henry Boyd was "a man of mark" in the late 19th and early 20th centuries. His ideas—and the energy with which he implemented them—were ahead of his time.

The Reverend R.H. Boyd's religious and business activities became inseparable, and his philosophy that church-related agencies should promote businesses and economic development in black America presented no paradox for him. Boyd believed churches and fraternal institutions should actively be involved in promoting Negro business enterprise for the uplifting of Negroes. He also believed the National Baptist Publishing Board should supply all needs and services to affiliate churches and give leadership through Christian education, training programs for church leaders, and promotion of home mission work. Between 1905-1906, R.H. Boyd organized the first National Baptist Sunday School Congress for Negroes in order to become a "beacon light" of Christian education for training church workers and children across America. In this Sunday school work, R.H. Boyd gave the Negro Baptists a national and international dimension, as well as a connection to white Baptists doing the same work.

In a way, Boyd was a Pan-African advocate because he tried to connect the Negro Baptists with those in the Caribbean and West Indies. From 1896 until 1915, Richard Henry Boyd headed the denomination's Home Mission Board; and he extended the board's mission work to the Caribbean where he organized and built several churches and a school building. On the national level, he and the NBPB assumed publication of the *National Baptist Union*, to combine it with the NBPB's *Review* to produce the popular weekly religious news, the *National Baptist Union-Review*. Thus, he hoped to unify the Negro Baptists across the country.

R.H. Boyd helped set the precedent for the NBPB to be involved in social activism that was increasingly prevalent during America's Progressive Movement—an urban reform movement lasting from 1890 through 1915. Some of the NBPB's publications obviously showed involvement in the Negro's struggle against Jim Crow laws, racial oppression, and conceited discrimination against Negro citizens. During the Negro's first literary renaissance, 1890-1915, the National Baptist Publishing Board contributed by printing and distributing many books by black writers. R.H. Boyd organized the Boy Cadets and the Girls Doll Clubs to involve the Publishing Board and its Christian education program to build character and leadership in youngsters in order to counter rising juvenile delinquency in early 20th century Negro communities. This cadet work also was a way the NBPB supported America's world war efforts within the Christian arena. Boyd and the NBPB assisted the Woman's Auxiliary of the Negro Baptist denomination with its mission work, and they helped the Women's American Baptist Home Mission Society's Fireside School with its efforts to import Christian education into local homes by printing the mission's *Hope* magazine. Boyd initiated cooperative mission work between the Negro Woman's Auxiliary and the Southern Baptist Convention's Women's Home Mission Board.

Through the leadership of R.H. Boyd's eldest son, Henry Allen Boyd from 1922 until his death in 1959, the National Baptist Publishing Board remained a viable and ever-expanding business in religious publishing. Many affiliated companies, such as the *Nashville Globe* were started by R.H. Boyd and others, had to be closed in the face of stiff competition in post World War II America. However, Henry Allen's continued involvement in Citizens Bank, which his father and other local entrepreneurs had started in 1904, grew the institution into a million dollar bank by 1946. Henry Allen Boyd expanded the Sunday School Congress into a massive operation resembling today's Sunday School Congress. This evolved from meetings that were dependent on housing in churches and private homes, into a gathering of tens of thousands of Baptist messengers housed in the nation's largest hotels and convention centers. The latter development came on the heels of the Great Migration to the North and the abolition of Jim Crow laws in the South that resulted from the Civil Rights Movement.

It was around this time when R.H. Boyd's grandson, T.B. Boyd, Jr. took the reigns of the company in 1959. He expanded it into a million dollar-plus corporation, and he built the company's first modern plant and headquarters in 1974. His was a feverish 20 years that saw the NBPB make a sudden leap into the modern business world.

Upon Dr. T.B. Boyd, Jr.'s death in 1979, his son, the great-grandson of R.H. Boyd, Theophilus B. Boyd III, took the reigns of the National Baptist Publishing Board and rapidly expanded the institution into a multimillion dollar business to include training, workshops, other services, and religious printing and publishing. If the NBPB would have moved at a slower pace, then the company indubitably may have emaciated and disappeared in the face of stiff competition and modern techniques of marketing, production, sales, and financing in the new American market economy; however, Boyd III took the company to new heights by its 100th anniversary.

Also in 1996, T.B. Boyd III decided to organize a new company, the R.H. Boyd Publishing Corporation, in order to complement existing operations and serve as distributor and marketer of printed materials, services, and programs. After being established in 2000, the R.H. Boyd Publishing Corporation sought new ventures into for-profit, nonreligious printing and publishing. This publishing house was born on a fast track in 1896, and its leaders never looked back while refusing to be a relic in a keen and highly competitive business. For more than 100 years, the R.H. Boyd Publishing Corporation and its predecessor, the National Baptist Publishing Board, has had only four presidents—all from the R.H. Boyd family.

— Bobby L. Lovett (August 17, 2006)

Dr. R.H. Boyd

CHAPTER ONE

Genesis:

The Early Life & Times of Richard Henry Boyd:

1843–1895

Prayer is the grace that seasoneth all. Prayer moves the hand that moves the universe; it knocks the door open; and like Jonathan's bow returns not empty.— *Richard Henry Boyd*

R ichard Henry Boyd (1843-1922) began his life as a slave on March 15, 1843. He was the firstborn child of a 23-year-old slave woman known as Indiana, who simply named him "Dick," short for Richard. Perhaps Indiana named the baby after a relative as was customary among slaves, such as his grandfather, or she may have given the boy his father's name. Indiana, or Ann (1820-1915) was born in Petersburg, Virginia, the youngest of 16 children born to slaves Dick and Mollie. Around age 7, Indiana was sold to slave traders, who carried the child further south to Columbus, Georgia, and sold her to Martha Gray. During this time it was socially fashionable for white women to have a personal servant—a "cute child"—they either owned outright or had received as a gift from their father or husband.

Martha Gray's family soon moved young Indiana from Georgia. It was common practice for slave-holding families to steadily move westward in seeking more fertile land that would support their growing slave operations. Around 1835, the Gray family moved to Noxubee County, Mississippi, which was part of the Western Territories ceded to the Americans by the British in the 1783 treaty that ended the American Revolution. This specific part of the territory below Tennessee had been admitted into the Union as the State of Mississippi on December 10, 1817. The State of Virginia furnished the fourth highest number of settlers to Mississippi.

During the birthing of Indiana's baby—in a log cabin with a door and two windows encased with wood shutters—she probably went through rituals and traditions common to other slave women of the time. They were careful that the bed was not placed "crosswise of the world" (north/south), but faced the east/west natural axis of the earth's rotation. Additionally, no one swept under the bed, because many slaves believed such activity was bad luck for the mother and the yet unborn child. Other slave women stood around the bed observing as the midwife did her job, making sure all rituals were in place to ensure good health for the child and the mother. Dick probably was subjected to other slave rituals as well: they likely tied a bag of ointment and herbs around his waist, across the navel to protect against diseases and infection, and placed a bracelet of beads around his ankle—a slave and West African practice of warding off evil spirits. Then the slave women would have prayed before presenting him to the rest of the slave community.

According to a photograph of an old slave cabin, which R.H. Boyd later said that it was like the one in which he was born, a fireplace was at one end of the room, and a hole in the floor gave access to a root cellar for storing food and hiding things. There was no porch, just a step where the cabin was raised a foot off the ground to allow the air to circulate beneath and to prevent the accumulation of germs and diseases. Without a porch, the slaves probably gathered around the front step where they conversed and transmitted community news. There was no vegetation of any kind around the cabin in Boyd's photograph, just dirt and a skinny shade tree at the back corner of the cabin. It is likely that the children gathered under the shade tree to play their games and engage in a childhood stolen by slavery.

According to established slave practices, Indiana would have been given a day or so to recover from child birthing before returning to the fields. The slave community would have given her as much respect and support as possible for a new mother, often doing part of her work if she felt weak and faint. Women made up the majority of slave workers in 19th century America, so Indiana's quick return to the fields was certain. She would have been allowed to return to the cabin twice a day to breast feed her baby, but when he was old enough, she would have harnessed him to her back, taken him to the field, placed him under a tree, and watched him as she worked in the fields.

When Dick Gray was about 5 or 6 years old, the Gray family and their slaves moved to neighboring Lowndes County in upper Mississippi on the Alabama border. Indiana gave birth to two daughters, naming one Mollie after her lost mother, and, in honor of her slave mistress, who had protected her since age 7; she named the second girl Martha. Under the age of 10, Dick and his siblings were allowed the basic life of children, not yet burdened with the work of slaves, but the master made sure the child's allegiance was to him and not to their parents. During these adolescent years, paternalistic masters would try to win a slave child's loyalty and affection that would last a lifetime.

Still seeking their illusive fortune, the Gray family edged their way closer to the vast lands of Texas, moving to Claiborne Parish, Louisiana. There, Indiana gave birth to a third daughter, Sallie. Dick, the only son, was about 10 years old and soon working as a "half-hand," according to the mechanisms and structure of that peculiar institution, slavery. In other words, they had him doing chores and taking food and water into the fields for the other slaves. Within another five years, however, he would have been treated as a "full-hand," working all day and producing as much work as the adult slaves. Owners expected slaves to pick 200 or 300 pounds of cotton a day, Monday through Saturday. The slaves were awakened before sunrise, marched to the fields to begin work at "can see," and expected to continue until "can't see." Then they began the walk back to the slave cabins, often not getting their cold supper until 9:00 at night. After that, they would do the chores required for taking care of themselves, their children, and other family members. Only then could they retire to a feather mattress or just several quilts on the cabin floor; seldom did slaves have individual beds. This routine was the norm except during the month of December.

Around age 15, when Martha Gray died and members of the Gray family divided her property among themselves, Dick was separated from his mother and three sisters. Benoni W. Gray assumed ownership of Dick, paying $1,200 for a prime slave hand. Indiana and the three girls went with a family to Houston County, Texas. Many other farmers also moved west after they wore out the land in the East; people called the abandoned, deep-gullied farms "gone to Texas farms." About 80 percent of the slaves taken to Texas and the Southwest were moved by their masters instead of by domestic slave traders as was Indiana's experience.

Benoni W. Gray's family moved to the fertile lands of East Texas in Grimes and Washington County, the western outpost of the Cotton Kingdom, about six counties west of the State of Louisiana. The *U.S. Census, Texas, 1860*, lists the Grays residing mostly in Grimes County: B.W., B.H., Elizabeth, James, Josiah, and W.J. Gray. By 1860, Texas had 182,921 Negroes and 420,891 whites, mostly Southerners. In some parts of East Texas, slave percentages of the total population ran from 7 percent to 73 percent. By then, Texas had 21,878 slaveholders, including 10,536 of them with large slave holdings. Slave owners were a minority, but they were the elite class, the plutocracy (wealthy class) in the South.

Because of his size, age, and intelligence, the Gray family gave Dick Gray a lot of responsibility, allowing him to pick up knowledge and skills that remained out of reach for most slaves. Without any knowledge of the whereabouts of his parents, like many other adolescent slaves, Dick accepted the paternalistic gestures of his white owners. They treated him in such a way as to gain his loyalty and make him content to stay on the plantation.

In the meantime, the slavocracy in Texas retained the confederacy's practice of human slavery and seceded from the Union on February 1, 1861. As Texas residents and slave owners themselves, the Gray family became involved in the heated debates that were leading the country into civil war. Master Gray and three of his sons put on home-sewn gray uniforms and joined a Texas Confederate regiment. Dick was 18 years old by then, so they took him along as their valet, which was customary among Confederate slave owners. The Rebels often impressed young slaves into military service. They drove wagons, dug fortifications, cooked, foraged for supplies, cleaned the camp, herded horses and cattle, raised the tents, took care of the rebels' personal needs during long marches, and moreover, assisted the surgeons in limb amputations and the disposal of human remains. Although the Civil War would last four years, 1861-1865, the Confederates may have bragged arrogantly about "whipping the Yankees," but they could not survive the power of a youthful America.

Master Gray, his sons, and Dick moved with a Texas regiment to the East to help stop the Union Army's march into the Upper South. However, the Union Army took the strategic state of Tennessee in February 1862, defeating the Rebels at Murfreesboro the following December. In 1863, the Union beat them at the Battle of Chattanooga and pushed them into Northern Georgia. Gray and two sons died near Chattanooga, leaving Dick to care for the surviving son who was badly wounded. Dick Gray accompanied his young master and likely other wounded Confederates back to Texas. In order to protect his young master who could have been charged with treason, they both stayed in Mexico for the remainder of the war. In the absence of Union occupying forces, parts of Texas were pillaged, burned, and terrorized by Confederate outlaws and ruffians. The Negroes in Texas remained isolated, and therefore, unaware of the Emancipation Proclamation (January 1, 1863).

Negroes in Texas also did not know that 179,000 Negroes served as U.S. Colored Troops (USCT) in Union Army cavalry, artillery, and infantry regiments, another 20,000 served in the Union Navy, and approximately 200,000 Negroes (men and women) served as laborers and in other noncombat jobs for the Union military agencies. Black Texans did not know President Abraham Lincoln visited the 25,000 USCT in General Ulysses S. Grant's Army of the James, just nights before General Robert E. Lee surrendered his Confederate Army of Virginia. The USCT were given the honor of being the first Union regiments to occupy the fallen Confederate capitol, Richmond, in early April 1865. In Texas, Confederates, slave owners, and other whites kept all of this glorious news secret.

Finally, on June 19, 1865, Union gunboats landed at Galveston, and the Union Army command sent the word through the Texas countryside that all slaves had been freed. Negro Texans began their emancipation celebration not on January 1 of each year—as most other freedmen did throughout the rest of the South, but on "Juneteenth."

By Dick remaining within the safety of the Gray family during these years, many things worked to his advantage. Some 486 Texan Negroes died at the hands of outlaws, thugs, and neo-Confederate raiders between 1866 and 1868. During the Reconstruction (1865-

1877), Negroes coming into Texas after serving in the U.S. Colored Troops could be singled out for harassment. Greedy landowners were doing all they could think of to nullify the Emancipation of 1865. They withheld land from the freed slaves, forcing them to sharecrop. They also forced some to sign apprenticeship agreements, which kept Negro orphans on the plantation until age 18 while the more ambitious Negroes were only allowed menial labor jobs with low wages. Moreover, many landowners terrorized the freedmen's white supporters and Negro civil rights leaders. Yet, according to a U.S. census, some 95 percent of freedmen stayed in Texas throughout the Reconstruction, concentrated mostly in the eastern counties.

After returning to Texas, in late 1865, Dick Gray worked and managed the Gray plantation, hauling bales of cotton with a team of oxen creeping at two miles an hour to the markets in Mexico. Dick Gray spent his young adult life in Washington, Grimes, and Montgomery counties until moving to the urban San Antonio area, near the Mexican border. He joined thousands of other Negroes who worked in the West as cowboys, driving cattle to railroad terminals, sleeping in the open, and working in dusty, wet, and hot conditions. He left this hard, low paying job and began working in a lumber mill in Southeastern Texas, becoming a foreman in Montgomery County. At age 22, he persuaded a local girl to teach him to read *Webster's Blue Back Speller*. She didn't mind teaching Dick as long as the Negro man paid her.

Under the protection of Union Army occupation of Texas and after the official Emancipation (December 19, 1865), many slaves wandered the roads in search of lost relatives. The more learned freedmen placed advertisements in local newspapers: "$25 reward for the whereabouts of Robert Porter, sold from Virginia to a Mr. William Robertson in Texas. Contact Mary Porter, his mother, in San Antonio." Like many other former slaves, Dick Gray began searching for his mother and siblings. Indiana and her family were in Houston County. In 1861, Indiana Gray had married Sam Niblett (Dickson). They had six sons: Samuel, William, Henry, Louis, Richard and Jim. Nine of Indiana's 10 children, except Richard Dickson who died in 1912, survived her. After finding her, Dick kept in close touch until her death.

In 1868, Dick Gray married Laura Thomas, but she died 11 months later. He joined the Hopewell Baptist Church in Navasota and was baptized by J.J. Rhinehart on December 19, 1869. Dick changed his name to Richard Henry Boyd, entered the Baptist ministry, and devoted his life to spreading the Gospel of Jesus Christ.

In 1871, R.H. Boyd married Harriett Albertine Moore. She was born a slave in 1855 or 1856 and came to Texas by way of Florida and Louisiana. After their marriage in Texas, she became R.H. Boyd's chief supporter, financier and business partner, although Harriett was unable to write. In the early 1880s, although much younger than R.H. Boyd, Harriett Albertine washed and ironed clothes to help send her husband to the nearby Bishop College in Marshall. This was a freedmen's school started in 1881 by the American Baptist Home Mission Society (ABHMS) of New York, which also established Morehouse College (Atlanta) and Roger Williams University (Nashville), among several other freedmen's schools. Northern missionaries wanted to educate Negro preachers so they could give leadership to freed slaves.

After two years, Boyd had to drop his college dreams and take care of their six-surviving children: Annie (1872), Henry Allen (1876), Martha (Mattie) (1879), Lugenia (Lula) (1883), J. Garfield Blaine (1885), and Theophilus Bartholomew (1894), according to data from the U.S. Census of Tennessee, 1900 (R-300) and the U.S. Census of Tennessee, 1910. Annie (Hall), named for her grandmother Indiana, who was also called "Annie," remained in Palestine, Texas, where she and her husband operated two funeral homes. Mattie (Bennefield) worked at the Publishing Board for five years after completing school. Lula (Landers) attended stenography school and Roger Williams University once the family moved to Nashville, Tennessee.

J. Blaine attended Virginia Union Theological Seminary, and later took a job at the AME Sunday School Union in Nashville. Theophilus completed Tennessee A&I State Normal School in 1914, where he was a star football player and described by the *Nashville Globe* as "a fantastic runner" for the winning A&I Tigers. Later, he was trained at the Morgenthaler Linotype factory in Brooklyn and spent his career at the NBPB. Henry Allen completed school in Texas and worked at the San Antonio Post Office before joining his father at the NBPB as assistant secretary, as well as managing editor of the *National Baptist Union-Review* and the *Globe* newspapers. Richard Henry Boyd was never able to return to college and complete his formal education, yet he received honorary doctorate degrees from Guadalupe College (Texas) and Alabama Agricultural and Mechanical State College.

In the meantime, Texas was readmitted to the American Union in 1870. However, the pro-Confederate Democratic Party gained control of the state in 1873 with a determination to keep the former slaves (about 25 percent of the population) beholden to the master race. In eastern counties, sharecropping farms comprised 25-80 percent of the total farms. Texas would be plagued by race riots, racial lynching, and the development of a corrupt and racist criminal justice system that left the Negro citizen in "a hard row to hoe." Churches became the freedmen's first and most influential of institutions, serving as places of refuge and even their political battlegrounds.

Reverend Boyd and other freedmen preachers became the most important leaders in the postslavery black communities. They began to organize their own district, state, and national church conventions and struggled to make these organizations independent of their white benefactors. In 1867, the Reverend I.S. Campbell was the first educated black minister to arrive in Texas. As a missionary for the Consolidated American Baptist Missionary Convention, he founded a church in Galveston and helped to form the Negro Lincoln Baptist Association in Houston. There would be 150 Negro churches and 12,000 members of those churches in Texas by 1880. The Texas Negro Sunday School Convention, which truly impacted the development of R.H. Boyd, began in 1880.

Richard H. Boyd organized churches in Waverly, Old Danville, Navasota, Crockett, Palestine, San Antonio, and Grimes City, among other places. He served as pastor of Nineveh Baptist Church in Grimes City, Union Street Baptist Church in Palestine, and Mount Zion Baptist Church in San Antonio. He also served as a district missionary between 1870 and 1874, traveling in a buggy as educational secretary for the Texas Negro Baptist Convention. Boyd and a white minister organized the Lincoln District Baptist Association in 1875. In 1876, at the American Centennial Celebration of

Emancipation in Philadelphia, Pennsylvania, R.H. Boyd was among the Baptist representatives from Texas that represented former slaves. *Frank Leslie's Illustrated Newspaper* (August 5, 1876) reported on the Centennial Exposition and the unveiling of the statue "The Freed Slave" in Memorial Hall.

In 1879, Reverend Boyd became a moderator for the Central Baptist Association of Texas. When his travels brought him face-to-face with Negro poverty, the dastardly conditions of the sharecrop system, and the awful dependency of the freedmen upon their former masters, R.H. Boyd preached that the Negro must become economically independent or return to a form of slavery dependent on whites. To gain some economic independence, so his ministry would not be hampered, R.H. and Harriett A. Boyd purchased as much land as they could afford in Montgomery County, San Antonio, and Palestine. Land was cheap in Texas, and Harriett and R.H. Boyd had the keen business sense to invest in it early. For Reverend Boyd, there was no need to separate the ideas of business and religion. Because of this, he impressed the freedmen with his industry business sense, honesty, articulation of the issues concerning them, and his organizational skills. These early experiences and philosophical developments would make R.H. Boyd a natural supporter of Booker T. Washington's self-help philosophy in the 1890s and early 1900s.

Boyd's fellow preachers, Sutton E. Griggs, Sr., Richard Abner, and Rufus Perry also believed Negro Christians had to make their own way and wean themselves from dependence on white Christian churches. This Boyd faction of Negro Baptist leaders (nicknamed "the separatists") wanted Negro Baptists to become learned, educated, and able to write and print their own materials. Griggs was a major leader in the Texas Negro Baptist Convention, which established Hearne Academy; Griggs, who was a friend to Boyd, founded *The Pilot*, a Baptist newspaper in 1867 at Waco. As far as Boyd and his colleagues were concerned, slavery was over, and Negroes had to assert their own independence by building and maintaining their own institutions to be competitive and equal citizens in America. After becoming pastor of Mt. Zion in San Antonio in 1891, R.H. Boyd hosted the Texas Negro Baptist Convention (TNBC) at his church. The Reverend Edward W.D. Isaac, pastor of

New Hope Baptist Church in Dallas, presided over the state convention. Like Boyd, Isaac argued that the freedmen and their descendants needed to rely less on white paternalism and move on with their own independence. Controversy developed at the 1891 state meeting with some members favoring a unified and highly centralized Baptist organization, while Boyd and others preferred a loose government association—a confederation—with much autonomy retained by local churches, district conventions, and related agencies.

The white Baptist missionaries were pushing Negro Baptists to centralize their operations, which was leading to future troubled waters. The American Baptist Home Mission Society (ABHMS) also wanted to consolidate some of its freedmen's colleges, including Bishop College in Marshall, Texas. This plan drew criticism from some Negroes, including several in Nashville, Tennessee, who opposed ideas to close Roger Williams University. Some delegates at the TNBC, held at Mt. Zion, favored the plan, but Boyd (who at the time was the educational secretary of the Texas convention) and other like-minded thinkers feared the Northern Baptists only wanted to gain complete central control over freedmen's colleges. The Boyd group believed Negroes had to remain separate and independent; to retain control over their own education was the only way that former slaves could truly transform themselves into free, productive, respectable, and *equal* American citizens.

Throughout the American South, since 1870, the formerly pro-Confederate Democrats had begun redeeming the Southern states from Republican control. Since the Compromise of 1877, the federal authorities had agreed to leave race relations in the hands of the states. Southern authorities imposed a vicious, merciless, unconstitutional Jim Crow system, which included separate education facilities between the races. This meant that Negro schools would be designed to be unequal and disastrous for the Negro's children, their grandchildren, and their future descendants. Jim Crow would use terror, lynching, and poll taxes to disenfranchise most Negro voters and render subsequent generations of American Negro children as intellectual cripples for the next 100 years. Boyd and his colleagues sought ways to overcome this fateful 19th century history.

The education controversy that began at Boyd's church was a serious issue. It continued for two years until 1893 when the Texas Negro Baptist Convention factions split. A "cooperationist faction" believed the Negro leaders should remain grateful and beholden to white church missionaries and their agencies that had assisted the freemen in their transition from slavery to freedom. Boyd and David Abner, Jr. led "the separatists" and formed a new convention known as the Missionary Baptist General Convention of Texas. The Reverend Isaac, Boyd's old friend, remained with the cooperationists and the Texas Negro Baptist Convention, which continued its allegiance to the Northern Baptists. Boyd resigned from Mt. Zion Baptist Church and became superintendent of Missions for the new convention. The Reverend H.H. Williams succeeded Boyd at historic Mt. Zion Baptist Church. The Northern white Baptist leaders, who toiled among the Southern freedmen, had strained relations with the independent-minded R.H. Boyd and other progressive-minded Negroes in the Missionary Baptist General Convention of Texas. White paternalism dictated that Negroes should follow the advice of their white friends.

Boyd believed that Northern Baptist organizations, such as the American Baptist Home Mission Society (ABHMS) in New York and their publishing arm, the American Baptist Publication Society (ABPS) in Philadelphia, had taken active roles in the controversy that split the Texas Negro state convention. Boyd instructed the Northern Baptists in Dallas to request that ABHMS missionaries and ABPS colporteurs not interfere with Negro Baptist affairs. This brash move by the former slave ensured an era of bad feelings between him and ABHMS officials.

The Missionary Baptist General Convention of Texas began to distance itself from the Northern Baptist agencies. A few of the separatists, including Boyd, believed the General Convention and its agencies needed to move closer to the white Southern Baptist Convention's local officials and churches—despite their affinity to maintain Jim Crow. In this regard, Boyd became a true racial accommodationist, often overlooking the racial practices of Southern white leaders while trying to gain concessions for the Negro people. Reverend Boyd thought of the Southern Baptist Convention as an alternative source for printing and distributing church literature to

Negro churches, and he soon used his old Confederate contacts to intercede on his behalf with the Southern Baptist Convention's Sunday School Board in Nashville, Tennessee. His slave background and racial accommodationist posture made it easy for Richard H. Boyd to cross the racial divide whenever necessary.

The Southern Baptists had broken away from the American Baptist Publication Society and began its own publishing board in Nashville in 1891, headed by James Marion Frost. The ABPS, which had printed American Baptist materials since 1824, wanted to maintain just one publishing house for all American Baptists and naturally opposed Frost's efforts to publish for Southern Baptist churches. Frost said that he was sympathetic with the ABPS and appreciated its work, but he would not work against this new movement of the Southern Baptists. Many Southerners were "still fighting the Civil War" and agonizing over the great defeat of 1865. At a great neo-Confederate meeting in Richmond in 1876, they opposed the North's "waving of the bloody shirt" and the boasting of their Civil War victories. As a result, former Confederates devised a patriotic movement of their own, even trying to resurrect the Confederate dead to make heroes of these men and their generals. The neo-Confederates and Southern patriots formed the Sons of Confederate Veterans Organization and soon proclaimed the South had a higher moral standard than the Northern regions. Therefore, few Southern white Christians were willing to reconcile with the North and were particularly unwilling to rely on Northerners (or "Yankees") for anything—including religious printing and publishing.

The Negro leader Frederick Douglass (d. 1895) was troubled by this neo-Confederate movement. Douglass said, "One cannot resurrect evil men from the grave and transform them into good men, because the evil they perpetuated in life lives on long after they are dead." In this milieu of postwar sectionalism and racial conflict, Richard Henry Boyd would take some advantages and opportunities to advance the Negro Baptists' cause.

In March 1895, Richard H. Boyd wrote a letter to T.P. Bell, the secretary of the Southern Baptist Convention's Sunday School Board in Nashville, saying, "The colored Baptists of Texas have not been accustomed to using your publications, but as I travel over the state, I hope to do much by way of introducing them." Boyd asked Bell to send some orders so he could teach the Sunday school superintendents and pastors how to place their own orders direct. "Our territory is very large and uses quite a supply of literature in the course of a year," said Boyd. Bell agreed to ship some church literature as a donation to Negro churches, but not as a challenge to the ABPS.

Early on, Boyd and his Texas colleagues realized that the Negro church and the education of former slaves were one and the same. Because of the high illiteracy rate of former slaves, there was no real separation of church and state. The few Negro public schools that existed in the Jim Crow era often were housed in local Negro church buildings during the week. Even some of the first freedmen colleges began in church buildings and were sponsored by church groups. During Reconstruction, the Republican Party meetings for Negroes and other political gatherings also took place in these church buildings on Friday and Saturday nights. On the seventh day, the church's Sunday or Sabbath school became a supplemental method of teaching adults and children how to read and write.

By this time, the Chautauqua Movement had begun in 1876 in New York. Northern missionaries spread the idea of training Sunday school teachers and making the lessons more educational. Boyd and the separatists endorsed this Sunday school idea. They used it on a small scale in the Texas Negro Baptist Association gatherings. Still, the materials were not under Negro control. Negroes needed to learn to write, print, and distribute Christian literature of their own choice and moreover, of their own thinking regarding theology and religious ideas.

On April 25, 1895, Boyd sent a letter to pastors, superintendents, and Sunday school teachers in the Palestine Association district, calling for a Sunday school executive committee in the Central Baptist Association to discuss church literature. They met at the True Vine Baptist Church in Navasota. The Reverend E.W. Adkins, president of the Sunday School District Convention, agreed to gather and send orders for Christian literature to Boyd, who would get the materials from the SBC's Sunday school publishing house. In May 1895, however, Reverend Bell became worried the ABPS would make a strong fight for its hold on Texas Baptists, white and colored alike. So, Bell donated $120 worth of literature for Boyd to distribute among Negro churches, but he held back official support of the Southern Baptist Convention.

A Negro Sunday school convention convened at South Union Baptist Church in Palestine the morning of Friday, June 4, 1895. The Reverend W. Waters moderated and the convention gave Boyd its support. The Sunday school convention used the Southern Baptist Convention (SBC) materials and held workshops such as "The Negro's Relationship to the Bible," "How Best to Teach the Bible to Grown People and Children," and other related topics. These meetings were Boyd's early conceptions of the National Baptist Sunday School Congress (1906–present). Through the summer of 1895, Boyd solidified his ideas and discussed them with pastors, teachers, and Sunday school superintendents. R.H. Boyd and his fellows attended the meeting of the American National Baptist Convention in September 1895. The meeting was just one more attempt by Negro Baptists to form a truly national convention. Negro Baptists, in the North and the South, had struggled for nearly fifty years to agree on an effective national denominational agency. According to William Hicks, *History of Louisiana Baptists from 1804-1914* (NBPB, 1914), by 1910, Texas would have 25 associations, 795 churches, and 69,950 members. Yet, fundamental problems still prevented unity for black Christians.

To better understand the foundation of history, upon which Boyd was operating, and upon which the Publishing Board was founded, one needs to revisit Negro Baptist history. Within this historical milieu of the frustrated Baptist fellowship, the NBPB would be born. The American Baptist Missionary Convention (ABMC) became the first Negro Baptist association, founded in 1840 and finally incorporated in New York in 1848. Only 10 percent of Negroes were free at that time and less than half of these lived in the North. When the ABMC passed an antislavery resolution at the 1859 national meeting, the few Southern Negro ministers in attendance, including Nelson G. Merry, a freed slave and moderator of the First Colored Baptist Mission in Nashville, were placed in a precarious position. Merry's mostly slave congregation was quasi-independent and controlled by the white First Baptist Church of Nashville. The white pastor was a slave owner and a leader in the proslavery Southern Baptist Convention, which had been founded in 1845 in opposition to the antislavery movement in the Northern Baptist churches.

In 1860, a number of churches in Connecticut, Maryland, Virginia and Washington, D.C., belonged to the ABMC. As Southern Negro churches became independent of their white masters' churches and drifted away during and immediately after the Civil War (1861-1866), the American Baptist Missionary Convention's (ABMC) roster of churches totaled 48 congregations. Another convention, the Northwestern and Southern Baptist Convention began at a St. Louis meeting in 1864 and included 26 churches from Arkansas, Illinois, Indiana, Louisiana, Mississippi, Missouri, Ohio, and Tennessee. They convened at Nelson G. Merry's church, which later gained its independence from the local white First Baptist Church of Nashville in August 1865. Merry's church gained a state legislative charter of incorporation as the First Colored Baptist Church of Nashville, Tennessee in 1866.

At a meeting of the two conventions in Richmond, Virginia, in August 1866, the ABMC and the Northwestern and Southern Baptist Convention united into the Consolidated American Baptist Missionary Convention (CABMC). They held their first official meeting at the First Colored Baptist Church in Nashville in August 1867. Richard DeBaptiste of Washington, D.C., became president. The Reverend Nelson G. Merry was elected vice president, as reported by the Nashville *Daily Press and Times* (August 17, 20, 1867).

After the Northern preachers were accused of mixing politics and religion in 1873, the Southern churches met at Nelson G. Merry's First Colored Baptist Church and formed the Missionary Baptist State Convention, including parts of Arkansas, Alabama, Kentucky, Mississippi, and Tennessee. The Southern churches mainly opposed any Presbytery-like governance structure in the national body as proposed by Northern preachers. Most Baptist preachers also opposed Episcopal structures and titles, such as "bishop" for their churches and ministers. The Southern Negro Baptist congregations had been mere extensions of white Baptist churches that held tight control of black Christians. After slavery and obtaining their independence, the Southern Negro Baptists preferred decentralized self-governance.

In August 1874, a group of Negro Baptist leaders formed the Northeast Baptist Missionary Convention. Next, the Southwestern and Southern Missionary Baptist Convention was formed at a meeting in Montgomery, Alabama, on May 29, 1875. In 1879, the Consolidated American Baptist Missionary Convention met in Cincinnati and dissolved itself, even though the Reverend Rufus L. Perry dogmatically continued the CABMC on paper until his death in 1895. Perry was opposed to relying on white Baptists in any way. R.H. Boyd and some other young Negro preachers would be pressed in his mold, believing white paternalism was bad for the progress of the freedmen. In many cases, as Frederick Douglass and W.E.B. DuBois would agree, white liberals helped the Negro "make progress" precisely because these paternalistic men also believed in the Negro's innate inferiority. For sure, most white Christians seldom demonstrated a belief in human equality; instead, they refrained from socially mingling with the Negroes—Christian or otherwise.

In December 1880, at a meeting in Montgomery, the Reverend William W. Colley and others founded the Baptist Foreign Mission Convention to assist in missionary work in Africa. Tennessee was represented among the ten states there, according to A.W. Wardin, *Tennessee Baptists* (1999). William H. McAlpin (d. 1905), who was born a slave in Virginia, presided over this convention for two terms until W.A. Binkley succeeded him. Because of the merger of associations in 1880, modern Negro Baptist Conventions often used 1880 as a founding date, yet they seemed to ignore the operation of the American Baptist Missionary Convention in the 1840s. Moreover, the founding of the Silver Bluff Baptist Church (South Carolina) by Negroes as early as the 1770s is completely ignored, lost, or strayed in African-American church history.

On April 5, 1886, from his base in Louisville, Kentucky, the Reverend William J. Simmons (d. 1890) called for a meeting "to promote piety, sociability, and better knowledge of each other" through a new national Baptist convention. Simmons was founder and president of a freedmen's school and author of a book, *Men of Mark* (1888). The book depicted elite Negro male achievers in the 1880s. Simmons also was a field worker for the American Baptist Home Mission Society (ABHMS). The Simmons' meeting convened in St. Louis on August 25, 1886, resulting in formation of the American National Baptist Convention (ANBC). Henry L. Morehouse, head of the ABHMS, assisted in the effort to unite the Negro Baptists into one national association with a central structure of governance.

With Morehouse and ABHMS officials as mediators, the new American National Baptist Convention met in Nashville, in September 1888. Along with the General Baptist Missionary Western States and Territories Association, a merger evolved. The meetings took place at the historic First Colored Baptist Church, even though Nelson G. Merry had passed four years previously. By the time of the meeting, the late N.G. Merry's congregation had suffered a bitter split under the new pastor in 1887, creating the Mt. Olive Missionary Baptist Church on Cedar Street in downtown Nashville. Mt. Olive later would serve as the home church to R.H. Boyd and family.

On September 26 of that same year, the Rev. Henry L. Morehouse addressed the gathering in Nashville's First Colored Baptist Church. In his address he said, "God hasten the day when narrow race feelings shall become less and less, being finally lost in the grander and all-controlling sentiment of Christian Brotherhood." The separatist delegates resented the presence of the northern white Baptists at the 1888 meeting. The idea of a complete and thorough merger of all Negro Baptist organizations into one huge convention failed. By 1890, they continued searching for an association model that was uniquely for Negroes and not influenced by white Christians.

The American National Baptist Convention (ANBC) remained operative and mostly under the control of the pro-Northern Baptist or pro-ABHMS/ABPS preachers. The Reverend E.M. Brawley presided over the ANBC until 1892, followed by Michael Vann, a preacher who was born in Madison County, Tennessee, in 1860. Vann became pastor of First Colored Baptist Church in Chattanooga and president of the ANBC in 1892-94 before dying unexpectedly in 1897. Vann was a great speaker. One of his sermons was printed in the *Baptist and Reflector* (1888). Elias Camp Morris of Arkansas was elected president in 1894. Meanwhile, by 1890, the Negro Baptists had two national associations: the Baptist

Foreign Mission Convention (1880) and the American National Baptist Convention (1886).

Additionally, the Baptist Educational Convention (BEC) grew out of a dispute in the American National Baptist Convention. In 1891, the Reverend Meredith W. Gilbert, pastor of Nashville's First Colored Baptist Church and successor to the recently ousted pastor after the 1887 congregational split, introduced a resolution to establish a home mission society. Some ANBC delegates, who were members of the Baptist Foreign Mission Convention, opposed the resolution and were joined by those endeared to the Northern Baptists' American Baptist Home Mission Society who also opposed the proposal. Pro-ABHMS/ABPS preachers opposed this independent move, as well. Whereas the ABHMS-affiliated American Baptist Publication Society (ABPS) only occasionally published a sermon or article by Negro preachers, M.W. Gilbert and other erudite preachers proposed the Negro Baptists publish their own magazine. To promote the importance of education, the Baptist Educational Convention (BEC) was formed in 1892. The Reverend W. Bishop Johnson became president of the BEC and began publishing the *National Baptist Magazine* on his own from Washington, D.C.

Ironically, the above three Baptist conventions met in the same city on the same days. This made sense because it saved money for members who belonged to one or more of the three organizations. They collectively agreed to meet jointly in September 1895. They intended to discuss a merger of the three largest national Negro Baptist conventions.

On the way to the Atlanta meeting, the Reverend Richard H. Boyd and his Missionary Baptist General Convention of Texas colleagues stopped in Nashville. They met with the corresponding secretary of the Southern Baptist Convention's Sunday School Board. Boyd told the Southern Baptist official the Missionary Baptist General Convention of Texas had given SBC literature to 12 of the 22 district associations. "If we do not start a series of our own," Boyd thought, "the Southern Baptist literature could spread throughout Texas." The Missionary Baptist General Convention's missionary board already had started a book depository with the Herald Publishing Company, which printed their minutes and other jobs. The Reverend Boyd suggested the SBC's Sunday School Board send church literature to be deposited there and drawn upon by demand from the Negro Baptist churches in Texas. The Southern Baptist Convention official said it would be good to have the convention's approval to avoid conflict with the American Baptist Publication Society. The Southern Baptists were not strong enough to start a fight with the better financed eastern establishment (ABPS) in the Baptist world. Boyd and the others understood the situation.

The Boyd delegation continued their trip to Atlanta, keeping the SBC discussions to themselves. The Reverend William D. Hemphill remembered being on the train with Boyd and the others when they had stopped in Nashville "to begin that monumental work of building a great publishing plant." Hemphill said, "We talked all night as we rode. He [Boyd] did not know then just what he was going to call the plant, but he said he was going to bring out Negro literature." According to the *National Baptist Union-Review* (December 21, 1946), before becoming a pastor in 1893, Hemphill had been a member of Boyd's church.

There were other developments and philosophies that would affect the milieu, which surrounded the birth of the National Baptist Publishing Board. In the fall of 1895, Booker T. Washington, the notable Negro leader and president of Tuskegee Institute, made his famous racial compromise speech at the Cotton States and International Exposition in Atlanta: "In all things that are purely social we can be as separate as the five fingers, yet one as the hand in all things essential to mutual progress." At the height of the Jim Crow era and in the midst of widespread lynching by white radicals in the South, Washington's speech essentially agreed to accommodate the whites' desire for social separation in return for economic and educational concessions to Negro citizens. The more radical leader, W.E.B. DuBois, eventually rejected Washington's accommodation philosophy, saying Negroes needed to have a "real college education" to train their "talented tenth" and promote integration rather than segregation. DuBois later elaborated on his ideas in the American classic he published, *The Souls of Black Folk* (1903). R.H. Boyd and most Negro preachers secretly agreed with DuBois; however, for the sake of survival and to avoid a race war the Negro could not win, they became loyal disciples of B.T. Washington and his racial accommodation philosophy. They called themselves "Bookerites."

The Negro Baptist denominational unity meeting took place on September 28, 1895, in Atlanta, where some 500 delegates and observers attended the sessions. During the Atlanta meeting, Negro Baptists agreed to merge into one national body, the National Baptist Convention, U.S.A., with E.C. Morris as president. In order to avoid the disputes from the old ABMC days and the issues of the 1888 meeting in Nashville, the NBC would not be an incorporated body and would not have an Episcopal structure. They would, however, remain a loose, unincorporated association, maintaining the autonomy of individual churches and district and state Baptist associations; otherwise, too many preachers, like the separatists, surely would vote against the merger. Among other compromises, a Home Mission Board and an Educational Board, respectively, would take over the functions of the Baptist Foreign Mission Board (1880) as well as the Baptist Educational Convention (1892). In 1899-1901, the National Baptist Convention, U.S.A. would add additional boards: National Baptist Young People's Union, Women's Auxiliary Convention, and the Benefits Board (to aid destitute and retired preachers). This "Great Compromise" would work among Negro Baptists for the next 20 years, although from time to time there would be some factional disputes.

At the 1895 Atlanta meeting, R.H. Boyd and colleagues bent the ear of several friendly delegates, but they did not say anything specific about establishing publishing operations independent of the white ABPS. The Northern Baptists had representatives at the 1895 Atlanta unity meeting just as they did at the September 1888 meeting in Nashville. The most influential Negro faction at the Atlanta meeting was beholden to the Northern white American Baptist Home Mission Society (ABHMS). Many of the pro-ABHMS/ABPS Negro preachers had attended freedmen's schools and colleges, including Roger Williams University, which were sponsored by the ABHMS. Many Negro preachers worked as representatives for the American Baptist Publication Society (ABPS), while others simply believed the Negro Baptists should remain loyal and dependent on the Northern Baptists. They believed the Northern Baptists had accomplished many things to help the Negro in the transition from slavery to freedom. Truly, these white missionaries had sacrificed dearly to help former slaves transcend from mere freedmen to citizens.

Boyd's Texas crowd, including the Reverend Hemphill, kept their mouths shut lest the unity meeting in Atlanta would break up and adjourn in an uproar. He and his Texas colleagues wisely kept the independent distribution and publishing ideas to themselves. Hemphill recalled Boyd had not clearly conceptualized how a publishing board could be established in affiliation with the new convention. At best, the new organization, the National Baptist Convention, U.S.A., merely was a loose coalition of the former three Negro Baptist national bodies: Baptist Foreign Mission Convention, American National Baptist Convention, and the Baptist Educational Convention. Churches in the Virginia area remained committed to the late Lott Carey of Richmond and his mission work in Africa. Although they were not yet a formal organization, the Lott Carey Baptist Convention focused its work on African missions and remained independent, despite the fact delegates from the Lott Carey churches in the east attended the meetings of the new NBC. Reverend Boyd had a dilemma; he needed affiliation with the new Negro Baptist Convention to monopolize the business of Negro Baptist churches. He also needed a publishing board that could maintain its autonomy as a nonprofit business.

Back home in Texas, in early November 1895, Boyd consulted his colleagues about carrying the publishing idea to the next NBC session. They agreed to help him begin the ground work of gathering support in Texas, which usually sent huge delegations to the annual Negro Baptist conventions. In early 1896, he held a huge conference with Negro missionaries and Sunday school workers in the new convention. Reverend Boyd even invited some local white Southern Baptist Convention preachers. The leading Negro Baptist conferees, including L.L. Campbell, W.B. Ball, and William Beckham, agreed to accept more Southern Baptist Convention Sunday School Board literature for the Negro Baptists' Texas depository. By July 1896, this experimental operation yielded an annual revenue of $2,000. Boyd and colleagues had no intention of relying on the Southern Baptists' Sunday School Board to supply them literature. For now, they needed the Southern Baptists. Likewise, the SBC needed them in order to break the Northern Baptist monopoly on Southern Negro Baptists churches without another religious war between Northern and Southern white Baptists.

There remained a major problem for the separatists—Southern white Baptists still promoted racial segregation. Nevertheless, Boyd knew that the Jim Crow-minded Southern Baptists had no problem with the Negro Baptists running their own affairs, associations, and agencies. The SBC decided soon after the Civil War to support limited educational efforts among the Negro Baptists and encourage the Negro Baptists to extend missions to Africa to "convert the heathen." Of course, some NBC delegates, especially the preachers who had been educated at ABHMS freedmen schools and colleges, vehemently opposed any contact with outwardly prejudiced Southern white Baptists. The Northern white Baptists, as liberal as they appeared, preferred paternalistic, cooperative arrangements with the Negro Baptists. Perhaps not as learned as they pretended to be, the Negro cooperationist preferred doing business with the less prejudiced Northern Baptists, although Northern whites had no desire to integrate socially with Negroes. Nonetheless, the Negro cooperationists argued that Northerners did not arrogantly display the awful "White Only" and "Colored" signs in public places as Southerners did. Negroes could vote unmolested in the North. Again, as aforementioned and referenced to W.E.B. DuBois, even white liberals and most white Christians in America, both in the North and in the South, held their racial prejudices based on a belief of Negro inferiority. Northerners never wavered from their Southern brethren about white racial attitudes. These two branches of "whites" in America differed in their methodology. They used different methods as well as unfair laws to maintain white exclusiveness and racial separateness.

The U.S. Congress passed the Morrill Land Grant Act (1890), which agreed to allow Southern states to receive federal funds to support agricultural land-grant colleges. Even if they established separate public colleges for Negro and white citizens, the law supported the endeavors. Next, in the case of *Plessy vs. Ferguson* (1896), the Supreme Court declared that separate transportation seating by race did no harm to Negro citizens as long as the separate accommodations were equal. In the Spanish-American War (1898-1899), whites from the North and the South fought side-by-side, allowing the Southern ideas about race relations to gain momentum in the national debate. These developments made Booker T. Washington's racial accommodation policy seem to be common sense to those designated as "whites" in the North and the South. Northern philanthropists began to invest their money in "separate but equal" Negro education as a way to continue uplifting the former slaves and freedmen while placating the segregationist South.

Again, Richard H. Boyd and his colleagues adhered to B.T. Washington's accommodationist racial policy. The harm in adhering to accommodationism as part of the strategy to uplift the former slaves was detrimental to the social situation. It encouraged European Americans' racial prejudices and their desire to maintain the exclusivity of being labeled "white and privileged above all other Americans." Yet, the Negro leaders were doing exactly as any racial accommodationists or Bookerites would do. They were trying to advance the Negro's cause in a near impossible racial environment where the alternative might have been a race war the Negro could not win. Boyd and his separatist group faced irony. They had to make use of the Southern white Baptists, regardless of their notable racial prejudices, in order to fight off the paternalistic grip of Northern white Baptists. Out of political necessity, the "separate but equal" doctrine of *Plessy* (1896) was the rally cry for the separatists and other Bookerites. Although one could not label them Bookerites, the leaders of the National Association for the Advancement of Colored People (NAACP) based their early federal court challenges against Jim Crow upon *Plessy vs. Ferguson*, claiming the South had violated the "separate but equal" principle. It was, after all, a thoughtful anti-Jim Crow strategy at a critical time in African-American history.

First Staff for the NBPB, 1896 ▶

▼ Book Bindery

◀ M & G Group
in Texas

◀ Rev. William Marion

Margaret V. McKicken ▶

◀ Meharry Dental & Pharm. Hall

Meharry Medical College ▶

◀ Meharry Nurses

Monuments of
R.H. Boyd ▶

CHAPTER TWO
1896–1905:
Early Years of the
National Baptist Publishing Board

The Negro must furnish his Sunday school with religious knowledge, his choirs with music, and his firesides and parlors with
wholesome literature, written and manufactured by his own
energy . . . Whatever is taught in the Sunday schools of this generation will be the doctrine of the church in the next generation.

— *Richard Henry Boyd*

Because of Richard H. Boyd's decision to use Southern Baptist
Convention (SBC) church materials instead of doing business
with the Northern agency, the American Baptist Publication
Society (ABPS) placed him on a road of no return, making Negro
Baptists independent of paternal control. This decision, like the split
in the Texas Negro Baptist Convention, also would reap enemies for
Boyd and any enterprises with which he associated. This conflict of
interest would spill over into the newly organized National Baptist
Convention, U.S.A. (cited as NBC hereafter).

After months of discussion with his colleagues in the Missionary
Baptist General Convention of Texas, the "new convention," in July
1896, Boyd rode the trains to Helena, Arkansas, home of Elias C.
Morris, president of the NBC. After spending time along the western bank of the Mississippi River, Morris agreed to Boyd's idea of
the Negro Baptists publishing their own literature. Elias Camp
Morris (1865-1922) was born a slave in Georgia. He worked as a
shoe maker and attended Roger Williams University in Nashville.
Later, he worked as a preacher, missionary for ABHMS and ABPS,
and organizer of the Negro Baptist Convention of Arkansas. Morris
needed Boyd more than Boyd needed Morris because the new NBC

president wanted initiatives underway in order to reflect well on his administration.

At the September 1896 session of the NBC in St. Louis, Boyd was confident he had Morris' support. In order to secure Boyd a position in the NBC's leadership, the Texas delegation gathered enough support for him to be elected as the corresponding secretary (head) of the Home Mission Board. The Missionary Baptist General Convention and the Texas Negro Baptist Convention represented 125,000 members and a huge block of delegates, who, incidentally, made a united effort to ward off opposition to Boyd's candidacy. Though they were split into rival Baptist state conventions, they were still loyal to fellow Texans whom they recognized as "one of us." After all, they had struggled through slavery together—even until the delayed date of Emancipation: Juneteenth. They also endured the disappointing consequences of Reconstruction in Texas. For decades to come, black Texas Baptists remained the secret strength of the Boyd family, of the Publishing Board, and for the Sunday School Congress. Members of the Boyd family, although transplanted to Tennessee, would always be referred to by Negro Baptist leaders in Texas as "one of us, one of ours."

At the September 1896 meeting, after securing the leadership position on the NBC's Home Mission Board, Boyd convinced the board members to entertain a resolution for a Negro Baptist publishing house. The resolution was sent to a committee, including Boyd, Emmanuel K. Love (Georgia), and Charles H. Parrish (Kentucky). Love, who was head of a Baptist convention in Georgia, believed the Negro had to have his own institutions because the whites had imposed Jim Crow laws, racially separating them from society. The committee approved the resolution and sent it back to the board, but Samuel N. Vass (North Carolina), R.J. Temple (Mississippi), and E.W.D. Isaac (Texas) opposed the resolution. Only Isaac, a Texan, would ease his opposition over time.

Boyd influenced the Home Mission Board to appoint a five-person printing committee. They agreed to allow the committee to print and publish a series of Sunday school literature until January 1, 1897. Boyd selected friendly preachers and tried to designate men who lived close to his designated site: Nashville, Tennessee. The boards, after all, operated from the hometown of the head of that specific board. Boyd selected G.W.D. Gaines from Little Rock, J. Geter also from Little Rock, E.C. Morris of Helena, E.R. Carter from Atlanta, and J.M. Moore of Kentucky. As corresponding secretary, Boyd was allowed a salary, provided, of course, the Home Mission Board generated its own revenue. The NBC had no treasury. Boyd had until November to resign his position in the Missionary General Baptist Convention and devote time to the Home Mission Board.

Richard Boyd visited the National Baptist Publishing Company in St. Louis to view their operations. After learning from the manager the company was suffering because of keen competition from the ABPS, Boyd offered $3,000 for the operation, but the ABPS already had arranged to buy out the company. In addition, their manager refused to entertain any idea about selling Richard Boyd "10,000 pieces of literature with Negro imprints." The Reverend Boyd was testing the waters and precisely locating the positions of his opposition. He already had contemplated the Southern Baptists in Nashville were his best chance to get help establishing a Negro publishing house.

Back home in Texas, Boyd began to unfold plans for a Negro Baptist publishing house. In October, he attended the Missionary Baptist General Convention meeting at Fort Worth, paying homage to his power base. He respectfully resigned his superintendent of education position as well as his job as pastor. In San Antonio, he made preparations for his family to move. He obtained letters of credit from two banks and cash from his wife, Harriett Albertine Moore, who served as stewardess of the household. The Reverend Boyd then took a small canvass bag and boarded trains believed to be bound for Arkansas. Really, he was headed further east to Nashville, Tennessee.

American society was segregated by law in the South and loosely segregated by practice in the North. Mostly in the South and various times in the North, racial lynching, which reached a crescendo in the 1890s, was the radical whites' response to runaway miscegenation in the Old South. Before the 19th Century, most mulattoes (offspring of a black and a white parent) had white mothers. By 1860, 10 percent of slaves and half of all free Negroes looked "as white as any white man." During their marches through the South in the Civil War, the Yankees were startled and dismayed when encountering "white slaves"—Northerners demanded the Southerners clean up this problem based on "moral grounds." The real fear of the Yankee observers was either Southern slavery should be abolished, or white-skinned persons could become America's slave workers. Thus, upon the freeing of four million Negroes after 1865, any rumors of sexual association between white women and black men was enough cause to cry "rape" and form a lynch mob. This violent racial environment ironically facilitated efforts by Boyd and his colleagues to establish separate, Negro controlled institutions where they could command respect and operate without fear. Negroes increasingly had to develop a "world-within-a-world." After all, the whites (North and South) wanted their exclusive society cut off from all other Americans, particularly from the American Negro.

Richard H. Boyd had to be very careful. "The cooperationists" wished to maintain the paternalistic strings to the Northern white Baptists, particularly to the ABHMS and the ABPS. The cooperationists continued to brand Boyd and others who wished to establish an independent Negro publishing house as the "separatists." The cooperationists continued to complain the separatists were destroying good race relations with the most friendly of the white Baptists and "being ungrateful to our Northern white friends at a time when the Negro really needed sincere white friends." The question was: Were any 19th century whites the sincere friends of the Negro? In this dangerous and turbulent milieu, the Reverend Richard H. Boyd continued his quest to establish a Negro publishing house. Boyd meant to accomplish and maintain the new enterprise independent of white paternalism and benevolence.

On October 15, 1896, Boyd met with the Reverend J.P. Robinson in Little Rock and quietly discussed the concept of a Negro publishing house. They agreed to schedule the meeting of the printing committee for November 4. Lack of a quorum forced the meeting to open on the next day at the offices of the *Baptist Vanguard* (Little Rock), with Boyd, Gaines, and Geter in attendance. Geter had converted to the Holiness Church. Precisely in the mid-1890s, the Pentecostal and Holiness movements were beginning to gather steam under Negro religious leaders in the nearby Memphis area. The following day, November 6, 1896, Boyd took a train east to

Memphis, staying with the Reverend T.J. Searcy of Beale Street's First Baptist Church (1866-?). This was the most historic brick church building in Memphis. After breakfast and discussions with Searcy, he took the midday train to Nashville, where Boyd spent the night at Reverend Charles Henry Clark's home near Gay Street.

Clark was pastor of Mt. Olive Missionary Baptist Church (1887-?) on Cedar Street. He succeeded the founding pastor, Thomas Huffman, in 1892, and increased the congregation of 200 to 300 members to 1,800 members. The Mt. Olive Church was incorporated in February 1897. They built an edifice at the corner of 9th and Cedar streets, only a block from the First Colored Baptist Church. Mt. Olive members held fairs and picnics to raise money for the church building. With the money they bought building materials, such as, lumber, bricks, and eggs to make mortar.

Charles H. Clark was born on October 15, 1855, in Christian County, Kentucky. His father, Jerry Clark, served in the U.S. Colored Troops of the Union Army and encouraged his children to enroll in school and "think like revolutionaries." After joining Green Hill Baptist Church, becoming a church clerk, deacon, and licensed preacher, Charles Henry Clark taught school before marrying Maria Bridges and having five children: Grant, Marie, Mary, George, and Willie. He served as the pastor of a church in Kentucky before accepting the Nashville job. Clark remained Boyd's right hand man and friend for the next 26 years.

On the next morning, November 7, 1896, Clark arrived from a trip to Kentucky, had breakfast with his surprise guest, and discussed the publishing plans. Clark then escorted Boyd to see C.S. Smith at the African Methodist Episcopal Sunday School Union publishing house. The African Methodists offered help and provided access to their printers. They also went to see James M. Frost at the Sunday School Board. Frost agreed to Boyd's plans, offered some plates for printing SBC literature, and took Boyd to see his printers. Finally, Boyd needed the printing committee to convene and approve the plans in order to take the publishing idea from its Texas beginnings to a national clientele.

In order to reconstitute the printing committee, Boyd replaced J.M. Moore with Clark. Next, Boyd took a train to Chattanooga and gained Michael Vann's support. Afterwards, he traveled to Atlanta to see E.R. Carter, who agreed to allow Vann to replace him on the printing committee. While in the area, Boyd took a train to Birmingham to see the Reverend Lewis G. Jordan and visit the Negro Baptist Convention of Alabama, which was in session. The ministers raised $27 for Boyd's travel and rushed him out of town before S.N. Vass (a field representative for the ABPS) heard about the publishing plans. Boyd stopped in Chattanooga and had Vann agree to arrive in Nashville by Tuesday. Vann still had influence as a former president of the American National Baptist Convention. In Nashville, Boyd preached at Mt. Olive. The next day he met with Frost and the printers. Lastly, Boyd asked J.M. Frost for a letter of support; Frost agreed to the request.

When the printing committee convened, a letter was received from Gaines saying he could not attend the meeting. Boyd replaced him with a proxy and appointed William Cansler, secretary of the Tennessee Negro Baptist Convention, to take Geter's seat. Cansler, who died in August of 1907, was a college graduate and a trustee of Roger Williams University, an NBC officer, and head of the mail department at the National Baptist Publishing Board. For many years, he was clerk at Pleasant Green Baptist Church and secretary of the Stones River Baptist District Association.

At 10:00 a.m. on November 11, 1896, the committee opened for business with a prayer. Shortly after prayer, the committee agreed to elect Clark as temporary chairman and Boyd as secretary-treasurer of any publishing venture. The prayers of both Boyd and Clark had been answered. After Boyd read Frost's letter of support, the printing committee voted to establish "the National Baptist Publishing Board."

Following a week at Clark's house and conferring with Frost and the printers, Boyd rented a room at the home of the pastor of Summer Street Baptist Church. Boyd revealed he had letters totaling $6,000 worth of credit from Texas banks, secured by land owned by his family, and $1,000 in cash, which Harriet had given him from her brother's lawsuit settlement. R.H. and Harriet Boyd owned a 100-acre farm in Longstreet, properties in San Antonio, 12 lots and a funeral home in Palestine, and some property in Spokane, Washington.

In the parlor of the Summer Street Church pastor's house, Boyd established a temporary office, using the pastor's secretary, Lula I.

Hobson. Boyd also discussed his plans with Allen D. Hurt, pastor of the First Colored Baptist Church and an official in the Tennessee Negro Baptist Convention. Hurt introduced Boyd to church member, Lena Randal (DeMoss). Before long, she started working for Boyd, which began her long career with the NBPB.

Boyd rented two rooms in the Brown Building at 408 Cedar Street (Charlotte Avenue), in the heart of the Negro business district. From there, he began operations. The printer agreed to print 60,000 pieces of stationery (letterheads and envelopes) with Boyd's handwritten signature printed on the paper. Boyd agreed with another company to have them print thousands of intermediate and primary quarterlies, and 80,000 primary and intermediate leaflets. He said, "I am secretary of the Home Mission Board of the NBC, and that board has not one dollar in its treasury; hence, they have not put one dime in my hands. As to the publishing committee or board, as we are now going to call it, I suppose if it were put to a vote today in the convention, it would be voted down by an overwhelming majority." The printing company agreed to let Boyd pay the bills until January 15, 1897. He really was holding back his credit and cash for other expenses.

At another printing company, he bought blank order forms, ledger books, pens, pencils, ink wells, and supplies. Next, he asked the local telephone company to install a telephone in the hallway of the three-story Brown building. By allowing the other tenants to use the phone for pay, Boyd could cut the cost of the telephone bill. Another trip to a different printing company produced 72,000 copies of publications, periodicals, and covers, with "National Baptist Publishing Board" imprinted on them.

One of the printers took Boyd to his bank to open an account, assuring him he would be treated equally. At the time, there was no Negro bank in town, and the white banks often treated Negro customers with utter disdain. Seven years later, R.H. Boyd and other local Negro businessmen in Nashville would remedy this situation by organizing a local Negro bank. At the end of that long November day in 1896, Boyd returned to his place of residence. Because it was late in the day, he gave Lena Randal money to catch the electric streetcar home. Boyd retired and fell asleep in his home office.

The next day, R.H. Boyd returned to work at the Brown Building only to find the generous offerings of several people. One resident, attorney T.G. Ewing, agreed to have the telephone number placed in his name. Charles Cansler brought over a lamp and two split-bottom chairs, and a deacon from Mt. Olive donated a table. Morris arrived by train to confer with Boyd, who took the president of the NBC to see Frost and the printers. Morris reminded all of them the NBC had no funds. Morris did not know Boyd had letters of credit and cash to pay the bills. Boyd knew from his experience in working with Baptist associations in Texas that convention officers should be prepared to pay any bills they incurred, whether in the name of the denomination or not. The convention would take claim to the results, but it was unwilling to pay the cost. As soon as he returned to Helena, Morris contacted A.J. Rowland, head of ABPS— perhaps as a professional courtesy—and briefed him about the publishing operations Boyd was starting in Nashville. Instead of being ambassadorial or harmonizing, Rowland was furious. Somehow, the guardian pro-ABPS Negro preachers, field secretaries, and missionaries had allowed R.H. Boyd to outflank them.

Richard Boyd employed a brick mason to build a window in a dark room at the Brown Building. Lena worked in Ewing's office during the two-day construction project. The NBPB offices officially opened in two rooms, with two chairs, a pine table, an ink well, and a few pencils and pieces of paper. One of the printers sent over another desk, asking Boyd only to pay the drayman. Boyd telephoned Henry Allen, asking him to send a typewriter and two quilts. Before each work day, Boyd would kneel and offer prayers to God. When Lena discovered his ritual, she insisted on joining him. This began the tradition of prayers and chapel at the National Baptist Publishing Board. To save money, Boyd moved into the publishing house. He slept between the quilts on a cot, cooked bologna sausage over the open grate, and washed in the building's restroom. Other struggling Negro professionals did the same thing in the Brown Building. In later years, they laughed about the "old days and hard times."

Within days, the envelopes, letterhead, and order blanks arrived from the printing company. The superintendent of the Summer Street Baptist Church Sunday School donated a chair for Boyd's desk. He and Bob Woods came to work at the NBPB and remained there for the next nine years as fireman and engineer. The dentist in the Brown Building, J.B. Singleton, brought back Lena's friend, Julia McKinney (Singleton), an experienced worker at the Methodist Publishing House, to help speed up the folding and mailing processes. Lena also brought aboard Lillie Lawrence, daughter of Emmanuel M. Lawrence (pastor of Kayne Avenue Baptist Church and a trustee for Roger Williams University), to help address 5,000 envelopes.

The small staff stuffed envelopes and mail bags. The letter from Boyd asked the "Pastor or Superintendent to read the letter or pass it on." It read:

> The Negro Baptists have been saying for six years that we need a publishing house of our own . . . I enclose you an order blank and envelope with the name and price of all our periodicals. Will you order at once and try them this quarter? [Here's] praying, hoping, trusting, and believing that the return mail will bring the order from your Sunday school. R.H. Boyd, Secretary of the N.B.P.B., Nashville, Tenn.

The Reverend Boyd took the nickel streetcar to the post office, gave the lady $50 for stamps, and sent the bags of letters to various destinations. The postal clerk and observers were amazed to see this Negro man with mail bags across his shoulders, and perhaps more impressed by the $50 he used to buy stamps. Did the observers know this was the beginning of the National Baptist Publishing Board, which would last for more than 100 years? Around December 15, 1896, the printers had the first publications delivered to the Brown Building. Boyd and the small staff worked through Christmas, wrapping and mailing orders. He hired I.J. Jordan to help ship the materials. Later, Jordan would become a missionary and salesman for the National Baptist Publishing Board.

On the afternoon of December 31, 1896, a box arrived by express mail from the family in Texas. It contained a Christmas dinner of turkey, baked chicken, pound cake, sweet tea, cakes, homemade light bread, and other goodies. The next day, Boyd invited the staff and building residents, particularly Singleton and Ewing who had been helpful in the operations, for dinner. They used wrapping paper as a tablecloth, offered a prayer, and served the delicious meal. Dr. Singleton and attorney Ewing, who also lived in their offices, appreciated the home-cooked food. Boyd had enough left-overs for two days worth of meals. This meal in 1897 began the traditional New Year's banquet at NBPB.

The January 15 deadline imposed by the Home Mission Board at the September 1896 convention was quickly approaching. On January 10, Boyd contacted Morris and informed him about the operations and bills owed. Morris arrived in Nashville, with a lawyer, Solomon Parker Harris, on January 15. Because Morris explained that Harris was brought along to help out, Boyd handed the man a broom and said, "Start cleaning the two rooms." Harris would remain at the NBPB, heading the bookkeeping department until 1915. Meanwhile, E.C. Morris surprised Boyd by calling a meeting of local Negro Baptist preachers to ask them for donations. Boyd surprised Morris and the group by saying the bills had been paid as of January 15. A puzzled Morris left on the train for Arkansas with a $50 expense check from Boyd. Morris was listed as "editor-in-chief" and received paid expenses during the commit-tee's meetings.

On January 15, 1897, the National Baptist Publishing Board began its first quarter of revenues and expenses. Boyd sent quarter-ly financial statements to the Home Mission Board chairman. After a spirited dash from Texas to Tennessee, R.H. Boyd had established a publishing house to service the Negro Baptist denomination. A few NBC preachers deeply resented R.H. Boyd's clever maneuvers to outflank them and establish a publishing company. In this loose association called the National Baptist Convention, the critics believed they had little opportunity to discuss a publishing board or define its relationship to the convention.

Although they had been taken off guard by Boyd's swift moves, some pro-ABPS Baptist newspapers, ABPS colporteurs, and ABHMS field missionaries spread the word about Boyd's printing operations in Nashville. Surely, many of them had received Boyd's classic letter. After learning the NBPB stamped materials really were Southern Baptist Convention Sunday School Board materials, the pro-ABPS *Dallas Western Star* said Boyd's efforts was done by "Negro backs and white man's brains." The *Baptist Herald*, edited by L.L. Campbell, defended Boyd's efforts. Few critics mentioned the

Southern Baptist Convention used private printers in the actual publishing of its materials. Boyd immediately decided upon two critical things: First, to move the infant company into closer relations with the Negro Baptist denominational organization. Second, he needed printing equipment and Negro writers to truly make the literature fit the Negro Baptists' needs. The old Texas depository arrangement would not work on a national level.

Boyd formed an editorial board, including Morris (Arkansas), J.T. Brown (Alabama), C.H. Parrish (Kentucky), W.A. Credit (Pennsylvania), C.O. Booth (Alabama), Mrs. M.C. Kennedy (Tennessee), Mrs. E.M. Abner (Texas), Miss M.V. Cook (Kentucky), R. DeBaptiste (Illinois), E.R. Carter (Georgia), Walter H. Brooks (D.C.), W.F. Graham (Virginia), J.L. Cohron (Missouri), Mrs. Lucy Cole (Virginia) and E.M. Brawley (Georgia). Boyd asked the editorial board members to write essays for the magazines and quarterlies. He also wrote letters to local Negro colleges asking them to take out paid advertisements in the NBPB's publications.

The Reverend Brawley had edited *The Negro Baptist Pulpit* (1890), which the ABPS hurriedly published in order to placate Negroes who had criticized the agency for not publishing articles and sermons by Negro Baptist preachers. Brawley, like Boyd and others, knew full well the American Baptist Publication Society (the Northern white Baptists) would not allow Negro preachers to publish their works and sermons in ABPS publications on a regular basis.

Boyd needed to visit the separatists and keep their support alive for an independent Negro publishing house, lest the cooperationists hinder his efforts in Nashville. Richard Boyd took this opportunity to visit his family in Texas in February 1897. During his trip, he stopped in Memphis, Little Rock, Texarkana, Palestine, Dallas, and Austin to distribute free NBPB literature and gain support. It seemed the opposition had found a way to impede Boyd's plans. Two days after arriving home, Boyd received an urgent telegram: "Return to Nashville, immediately!" Samuel P. Harris sent the telegram because one company had not printed the requested materials. Richard Boyd would have to return later to move his family from Texas to Nashville. On his rush back to Nashville, Boyd stopped at Guadalupe College to visit one of his children. Afterwards, he stopped in New Orleans for a Baptist meeting, only to encounter S.N. Vass, who offered Boyd a position with ABPS on one condition: he would need to stop the publishing operation in Nashville. During his stop at Dexter Avenue Baptist Church in Montgomery, the members raised money to help Boyd's efforts. Therefore, Boyd began to see the Publishing Board as an effort for and by all Negro Baptists beyond the uncertainty of the National Baptist Convention.

When Boyd arrived back in Nashville, Harris said, "What shall we do about picture cards and Bible lesson picture cards?" Boyd calmly replied, "Let us not stop here to build bridges." After the meeting, Boyd kneeled and prayed. A telephone call from J.M. Frost informed Boyd that a publishing company in Boston had sent the Sunday School Board too many picture lesson cards. The next day, the National Baptist Publishing Board had picture lesson cards with "NBPB" imprinted on the front, ready for mailing.

Assuming whites would stick together on 19th century race issues, the head of the ABPS sent Frost a letter chastising him for helping Boyd. Frost replied on December 8, 1896 saying, "I regret the tone and spirit which it manifests, concerning the movement of our colored brethren to publish Sunday school literature. If you knew the facts in the case, I am sure you would feel and speak differently." Frost read the harsh letter at the SBC session in Wilmington on May, 1897. He had it published in the convention's proceedings. Frost said, "We were glad to see them [the Negroes] undertake so momentous an enterprise, and earnestly wish them the greatest possible success."

For the first quarter in 1897 January 15–April 15, the NBPB had revenues of $1,774.06 and expenses of $1,518.77. The company circulated 180,000 copies of Christian literature that quarter. Boyd commended the staff, "especially my faithful cashier [Randal] who has been with me from the beginning, and my bookkeeper [Harris], who has laid the foundation for our future bookkeeping in this office. Now, we need a stenographer, another mail room, and a job press." By the second quarter, he had editorial essays from members of the editorial board to be printed in the *Teachers' Monthly* and the quarterlies.

At the September 1897 NBC session in Boston, Vann and Gaines agreed to present the printing report, sparing Boyd any attacks from his learned enemies. However, the Reverend Vann died, and Gaines was not available. Boyd gave the report and received surprising applause. His distracters found R.H. Boyd to be as intelligent as they were, despite his lack of a full college education. Still, their mockery of him would turn to outright hatred and disdain for his efforts to actually sustain a publishing house. However, A.D. Hurt joined the Home Mission Board, and J.P. Robinson supported Boyd's efforts.

In 1897, the Negro Baptists in the East, mostly from Virginia, who revered the late Lott Carey and his missionary efforts in Africa, now formalized the Lott Carey Baptist Foreign Mission Convention. These people needed white Baptists to financially support their African mission work. Because of this action, the Lott Carey group would be friendly to R.H. Boyd's publishing efforts. Years later, the Lott Carey Convention had cooperative, formal publishing agreements with the National Baptist Publishing Board.

Factionalism within the young National Baptist Convention, USA, worried President E.C. Morris. He later said,

> A considerable number of Colored Baptists have organized what is known as the Lott Carey Foreign Mission Convention, and this Board is doing the same class of work that is being done by our Foreign Mission Board. We concede the brethren have the right to do their foreign mission work independently of the National Baptist Convention, but it is neither intelligent nor wise to have such division in our ranks — *National Baptist Union* (September 27, 1902).

For the sake of good business practices, around August 15, 1898, Richard H. Boyd, the board members, and their attorney chartered the NBPB Company under the laws of Tennessee. The charter made the National Baptist Publishing Board a corporation which could sue and be sued, own and sell property, sustain its operations over generations, and select its own leadership. The original directors were Boyd, E.C. Morris, J.E. Knox, J.P. Robinson, G.W.D. Gaines, E.J. Fisher, C.H. Clark, and G.M. Moore. The operation no longer was a mere printing committee and a publishing company in name only.

Part of the charter read,

> The Board of Directors may have the power to increase the num-
> ber of directors...if they deem the interest of the corporation
> requires such increase; and they or any subsequent Board of
> Directors may have the power to elect other members, who on
> acceptance of membership, shall become... equal with the original
> incorporators.

The constitution also stated, "Five of the nine directors shall be residents of the state of Tennessee." The charter allowed Boyd's NBPB to perpetuate and protect itself from convention politics and interference. Charter and bylaws were sent to Robinson, the chairman of the Home Mission Board and reported to the NBC session on September 15, 1898, in Kansas City, Missouri.

The Home Mission Board agreed to consolidate the NBPB and the Home Mission Board operations; after all, R.H. Boyd was corresponding secretary and treasurer of both. At the September 1898 National Baptist Convention session, President E.C. Morris was able to say the following:

> Notwithstanding we were accused of issuing 'backs which cov-
> ered white men's brains,' in less than two years we are turning out
> more than 200,000 periodicals each quarter. We can no longer be
> regarded as mere consumers in the literary world but that we may
> be justly termed producers.

Boyd began using profits and his own money to buy printing equipment. He hired printers, such as Dock A. Hart. Joseph Oliver Battle, fresh out of Chattanooga's Howard High School, was hired as an errand boy. Boyd bought nearly $6,000 worth of printing equipment from printing companies going out of business. He sought to lease a vacant building used as a printing company, but the owner refused to accept the lease from a Negro. It was an unspoken code among Southerners that whites were to give Negroes no opportunities to become economically equal. The Reverend Boyd then secured a $10,000 loan at 6 percent interest in 14-year bonds to buy a large private residence on 2nd Avenue South. Soon after, he bought another building behind the structure. He later leased an old drugstore across the street and a small building in the alley. In these odd facilities, the National Baptist Publishing Board soon was operating in its own complex.

Harriett A. Boyd began to study and write in 1898 at the age of 42 while her husband, the 53-year-old R.H. Boyd, was busy building a publishing house. Harriet was quite independent and usually made her own money by taking in boarders before joining her husband in Nashville. Once the six children were of age and in school, Harriett turned her attention to herself. With the help of her teacher Katie Shelton, Harriett Albertine wrote one of her first complete letters. In it she articulated:

> God has helped us start a publishing house for our people. God has been with us these four years, and we believe He will guide us all the way, that the work may prosper. Pray for us.

Harriett Albertine Boyd wrote the letter to Joanna P. Moore (1832-1916), head of the Fireside School in Nashville. Moore later printed Harriett's letter in the Fireside School's *Hope* magazine (October 1900) as an example of a Christian woman advancing herself while maintaining a home and a wholesome Christian family.

In 1899, the National Baptist Convention held the annual session in Nashville. Morris answered criticism about a Negro publishing effort, saying, "It is they, the white Christians, who have drawn the color line." At the September 12-17, 1900, NBC session in Richmond, the Reverend W.H. Sherwood believed Negroes should support their own businesses. Morris said:

> The supplementary institutions planted by the colored Baptists do not seek to supplant those formed by our friends [ABPS], but rather to augment and enlarge the opportunities of and for our race. It is necessary . . . to develop the business side of the race.

Morris further stated:

As was expected, criticism came thick and fast, but our manager [Boyd], a man who lays no claim to an extensive education, was well prepared to receive all that came. And permit me to say that to his indomitable courage, coupled with his vast store of common sense, is due much of the success of that enterprise [the Publishing Board].

Despite not having the support of everyone in the National Baptist Convention, the NBPB reported to the 1900 NBC session. Boyd's report said the books had been balanced at $49,309.37. The convention even endorsed Boyd's *Pastor's Guide and Parliamentary Rules* book and directed him to publish a Negro Baptist hymnal. Since 1897, R.H. Boyd had been gathering hundreds of Negro songs. This was years before William C. Handy, "the father of the blues," began his work at an Alabama college and started to assemble rural Negro music into written form and published musical notes. The Publishing Board and R.H. Boyd became known as the "father of published Negro church music."

According to Richard H. Boyd, the NBPB became a mission for uplifting and educating Negro Christians. Boyd also wanted to teach children the true Baptist doctrine as well as instruct them to defend their faith, obey laws, participate in government, and be good citizens. Additionally, Richard Boyd made the Home Mission Board a reputable operation. After meeting with James M. Frost in Chattanooga on November 28, 1900, he persuaded the Southern Baptist Convention to sponsor two Negro missionaries for NBC Home Mission Board field operations. The close affiliation with the Southern Baptists would further anger Boyd's critics.

At a time when the Negro was engaged in his first literary Renaissance, the National Baptist Publishing Board contributed to the movement. The NBPB produced 24 book titles between 1900 and 1902. By 1905, the company had published even more book titles, including *The National Baptist Hymnal*, third edition (1903), edited by R.H. Boyd and William Rosborough. To avoid liabilities, the early NBPB preferred to own publishing rights instead of copyrights. The NBPB reported $2,423 in excess revenues in 1900 after buying new machinery and additional buildings. They used excess funds to aid the Home Mission Board activities and hire William Beckham as the traveling field secretary for the Home Mission

Board. Of course, Beckham, a Texan and a Boyd colleague from the early years, also promoted National Baptist Publishing materials in the field across the nation.

The Women's Convention, within the NBC, had become a recognized board in 1900. Boyd became the unofficial adviser to the women's group because the NBPB supplied them free literature and various funds. He helped persuade the Southern Baptists' Women's Auxiliary to give money to help the Negro Woman's Convention hire two home missionaries. Boyd and the NBPB gave the Negro women the matching funds. In addition, the NBPB published their newsletters. After the Women's Convention's executive committee visited the publishing house on June 2, 1902, they said, "Dr. Boyd is, indeed, one of the greatest men of the age. Our publishing house at Nashville should receive our hearty support by way of liberal patronage." The NBC women eventually built a missionary house in Africa and a school for girls in Washington, D.C. The NBPB continued to assist the Fireside School in Nashville, which was headed by female missionaries of the ABHMS.

After Boyd conceived the idea of a single newspaper for Negro Baptists, the NBPB assumed control of the *National Baptist Union*, a newspaper published by the Baptist Young People's Training Union, which had moved its office to Nashville and begun cooperation with the NBPB. Several Negro Baptist newspapers were published across the country, but none of them had national circulation. In many rural places, Negroes depended on black Baptist papers for their world news. The NBPB lost $1,601 on the *National Baptist Union*, but gained a wider audience. It also picked up more critics who believed Boyd was consolidating three Baptist entities under his control. When Boyd asked the 1902 convention for $10,000 to upgrade the NBPB's facilities and equipment, he received no money. Morris said:

> The impression has gone out that the publishing board is 'a money machine,' hence, many expect it not only to do their work for a small price, but expect the publishing house to aid them financially.

R.H. Boyd made the mistake of criticizing the American Baptist Home Mission Society. Boyd said the following:

For thirty years the Negro Baptists of this country have sustained most friendly relations to this society, and reaped from it labors of love and many profitable rewards. [But] the fact still remains that some of its officers have made serious and damaging mistakes in dealing with our people—*National Baptist Union* (December 13, 1902).

Boyd's remarks caused the Reverend H.L. Morehouse to issue a stern rebuke. Some NBC members claimed Boyd continued to hold a grudge against the Northern Baptists because of the denominational split in Texas and the old arguments over Bishop College. Meetings were called to cool things off, but the ABHMS really was angry about the NBPB's close relationship with the Southern Baptists. Boyd was advised by NBC officers to tone down the anti-Northern Baptists' rhetoric and work more closely with them as he did with the Southern white Baptists. Boyd said, "The races should strive in every manner possible to help each other. The [Southern] white man is our big brother in this country"—*National Baptist Union* (September 12, 1903).

By 1905, resolutions were introduced in the annual NBC sessions to separate the Home Mission Board from the NBPB's operations, even though the NBPB was the main source of money for the Home Mission Board. Things were left alone for the time being.

In 1905, Boyd and the Publishing Board conceptualized an annual Sunday school gathering on a national level to spread Christian education, distribute the NBPB's literature and products, train pastors, Sunday school superintendents, and educate children and young adults in the ways of the Baptist doctrine. Boyd and his successors understood and appreciated the concept of training Negro church personnel, children, and church members in the rudiments of Christian education and management of church affairs. They further were encouraged to do this in an organized fashion, partly as a result of their attendance at national Sunday school meetings and the Chautauqua.

The center for Chautauqua was located in New York State and scheduled during the summer to host and train Baptist missionaries, teachers, and leaders. It was founded at Chautauqua Lake, New

York, with the first assembly held in August 1874. The movement rapidly expanded to include a school of languages, a summer school for public school teachers, a school of theology, and a series of clubs for young people interested in reading music, fine arts, physical education, and religion. Chautauqua University lasted between 1883 and 1898. Tent Chautauqua programs traveled the country between 1903 and 1930. Negro churches and other church groups adopted the organizational methods of summer Chautauqua into their institutional programs of Christian education. Boyd and his son, Henry Allen, often attended national and international programs to promote Sunday schools and Christian education. Moreover, beginning in the 1870s and lasting for about 20 years, Richard H. Boyd had been a district and convention moderator for the Baptists in Texas. He organized many meetings on the local, district, and state levels to improve the education of church personnel. Because the National Baptist Publishing Board, now almost 10 years old, printed and distributed Christian literature, it was only natural the company use its resources to expand into the arena of educating adults and children in knowledge, skills, and methods for teaching Christian doctrine. No other church-related agency among Negro Christians was better prepared to do this—to emulate the Chautauqua on a national scale.

Additionally, the "Old Landmark" controversy was always alive. Young preachers and churches at the turn of the 20th century frequently drifted away from "true Baptist principles." Old Baptists often sang, "Let us all go back to the old landmark." Richard H. Boyd and his colleagues always worried many adult and young Negroes had minimal education. They could be easily influenced by unlearned preachers, who were ignorant about the Baptist polity but could easily capture an audience by emotionalism and empty rhetoric. Ambitious preachers could lead such a congregation to believe in religion void of doctrine based in the original Baptist denomination and its non-Episcopal structure. Some pro-NBPB preachers, including John S. Trower, began lecturing Negro churches about the need to rid Sunday schools of ignorance and for the necessity to have teachers properly trained in the Baptist doctrine. In the *National Baptist Union* (August 26, 1905), Trower said:

I am proud of being a Sunday school man, and I could not be a Sunday school man of the colored race connected with the Baptist denomination without at the same time being a firm believer in all racial possibilities, and therefore a believer in the ultimate grandeur of our [National Baptist] Publishing Board and its very excellent literature.

He advocated the "Model Sunday School." It's purpose was to "save our children from such [deep ignorance of] knowledge" about the Baptist faith and its religious practices.

In the 1890s and during the first decade of the 20th century, the Holiness and the Pentecostal movements were sweeping up Negro Baptists and other Negro Christians in the Tennessee and Arkansas areas. Bishop Charles H. Mason and others founded the Church of God in Christ, based on Acts 2:4, in 1895. About the time R.H. Boyd was establishing the NBPB in Nashville, the first General Assembly of the Church of God in Christ was held 210 miles away in Memphis in 1897. Those who believed in more fervent religious services, the speaking in tongues, and washing of feet broke with Mason and formed the Holiness churches consistent with the Pentecostal denominational tradition. Saint Mary Magdalena L. Tate (1871-1930) was a founder of the Holiness movement called the Church of God (1 Timothy 3:15-16). Around 1903, they established their headquarters in Nashville on Heiman Street, where the late R.H. Boyd's widow lived a few blocks away. Like the Pentecostals, the Holiness church had elders and bishops. The denomination would spread to some 43 states as well as Jamaica after the death of Mother Tate. She was reinterred in Nashville's Greenwood Cemetery (1963).

The Baptist Sunday school movement became popular with several church leaders. The Reverend Samuel N. Vass was lobbying the idea through the *National Baptist Union* (January 16, 1904). S.N. Vass proclaimed:

Of all the various agencies that have been fostered by the Christian church for the salvation and spiritual culture of young people the Sunday School easily takes first place and has the strongest hold upon the masses . . . It is the work of the Publishing Board especially that has made this one of the greatest conventions in the world. And yet the Publishing Board owes almost everything that it is to the Sunday Schools among Negro Baptists.

In the time of slavery, Negro Baptists had to attend church under the watchful eye of their masters. They relished the Sabbath School where they were exposed to the rudiments of learning to understand the Bible. Immediately after the Emancipation (1865), Negro Sabbath School often taught the alphabet, recitation of biblical passages, and reading out of the Bible by learned youngsters to the older freedmen.

After careful discussion, around late summer in 1905, R.H. Boyd and the NBPB conceptualized the "National Baptist Sunday School Congress" based on 2 Timothy 2:15: "Study to show thyself approved unto God, a workman that needeth not be ashamed, rightly dividing the word of truth" (KJV). Second Timothy 2:16 also warned against false teachings: "But shun profane and vain babblings: for they will increase unto more ungodliness" (KJV). Boyd instructed his son, Henry Allen, to begin work if he wished to finish by next summer. They would use their home church in Nashville to launch the first Congress. The session, like the ones Boyd operated in the district association meetings in Texas in the 1880s and early 1890s, was designed to bring together pastors, Sunday school superintendents, and teachers in annual meetings to discuss many things. Their talks centered around Sunday school lessons, issues affecting the church, and training teachers how to use printed materials to teach the Negro population, which still was mostly illiterate. This time, however, churches from across the country would be invited for a week of activities, learning, and teaching.

R.H. Boyd and his staff carefully thought out the scheduling and details of the first Sunday School Congress, which would remain steadfast as a tradition for a 100 years. To prevent conflict with the annual September session of the denominational convention, the National Baptist Convention, R.H. Boyd organized the Sunday School Congress in June. In Texas, the Negroes celebrated "Juneteenth." (Emancipation of slaves in Texas, June 25, 1865). In that month, they used June as the summer vacation period. Furthermore, the time between May and September was ideal because children were out of school, freeing parents to bring them

along to the Congress. The Congress would begin the week following the second Sunday, and thereby not conflict with the Fourth of
July, another important African-American holiday.

The NBPB's Congress would begin with a service in the host
church on the second Sunday, a parade on Monday, and a musical
on Tuesday evening to attract a large crowd. The main sessions
began Wednesday morning and ended Friday night. Boyd presented some of his ideas in September 1905 at the National Baptist
Convention as it convened in Memphis.

In the spring of 1906, Richard and Henry Allen Boyd sent out the
invitation for the first National Baptist Sunday School Congress. Henry
Allen Boyd coordinated most of the event, scheduling railroad trains to
bring the delegates to the host city, arranging for local families to house
the visitors (because Jim Crow hotels would not accommodate them),
putting the classes and program together, leading the "Congress
Parade" in the host city's streets, and coordinating the four to five day
event. Gradually, his title became "Congress Secretary." The *Nashville
Globe* and the *National Baptist Union* advertised the Congress event as
well as the railroad excursion rates. The Publishing Board printed the
program, hired and trained the teachers, and prepared and printed the
curriculum and books. The delegates or "messengers" would send
their names and addresses to Henry Allen, who would return the name
and address of the designated private home where messengers would
reside during the week of the Congress. Arriving messengers were
transported immediately to their assigned residence, paying the head
of household for their accommodations.

In June 1906, Richard Boyd opened the first Sunday School
Congress at Mt. Olive Missionary Baptist Church. All members of
the Boyd family, including his elderly mother and his young children, had roles to play in order to make the Sunday School
Congress successful and convenient for the messengers. Indiana
Dickson was happy to help because she loved to hear the messengers respectfully call her "the mother of the Congress." Charles
Henry Clark, chairman of the NBPB, set the precedent for the
chairman, always officially opening the Sunday School Congress
sessions. The first Sunday School Congress was small but successful. The Reverend J.H. Brown of Florida praised the new efforts of
the National Baptist Publishing Board:

Thirty years ago our Sunday Schools were a crude imitation of what we saw others doing. Our National Baptist Sunday school helps [literature] are standing the test of the age, and in every way meeting the demands of our workers and students —*National Baptist Union* (July 21, 1906).

R.H. Boyd learned many things while attending the International Sunday School Association meeting in Indiana, August 1906. There was an International Committee, which prepared lessons for the religious publishers. A World Convention for Sunday School workers was held in Jerusalem around this time, and the work was extended to Negro adults and children.

The involvement in the Sunday school movement brought even more national attention to Boyd and the Publishing Board. James E. McGirt of *McGirt's Monthly Magazine* (Philadelphia, November 1906) focused an article on the National Baptist Publishing Board, illustrating its staff and facilities. The offices were deemed the "six great buildings owned out and out by Negroes."

The "Second Session" of the Sunday School Congress was held in New Orleans (1907). The Reverend W.S. Ellington, editor at the NBPB, and members of his First Colored Baptist Church attended the "National Baptist Sunday Congress and Young People's Chautauqua at New Orleans"—*Nashville Globe* (June 21, 1907). The 500-mile trip to New Orleans was rough and traveled mainly on the back of Jim Crow railroad cars. Travelers required a day to recuperate. Still, the Reverend E.W.D. Isaac said, "In the midst of oppression and persecutions the Negro in this country has much for which to be thankful"—*National Baptist Union* (January 12, 1907).

When Congress arrived, the Boyd family boarded the "Congress Special" in Nashville, filled with guests and members of the other convention boards, and picked up other delegates at various stops. The Publishing Board officers and the National Baptist Convention officers usually arrived together. In the host city, the Congress secretary, Henry Allen Boyd, dressed in an immaculate white suit, white shoes, and a white straw hat. He led the "March for Jesus" parade. The Reverend Henry Allen Boyd amazed the spectators by dancing in front of several brass bands. He dazzled the crowd with his enthusiasm and kept their spirits up during the "March for Jesus." The first day's spectacle lifted interest and caused more local residents to attend the sessions held at the host church or local auditorium. The songs, the uniformed marchers, the NBPB's Brass Band, the huge Congress Choir, the participation of local Baptist churches, and Henry Allen Boyd's participation in the parade with his white shoes, white suit, and fine straw hat all were designed to attract attention and draw the local community to the daily sessions. Although the messengers were selected by churches, district congresses, and state congresses, everyone was welcome to register and participate in the classes and other activities.

The chairman of the National Baptist Publishing Board (1896-1920), Charles Henry Clark, opened the first day's sessions. The president of the National Baptist Convention was given the honor of speaking at the huge gathering. The audience gave cheers to the Congress Secretary (H.A. Boyd), and on cue they engaged the Chautauqua salute—three waves of the handkerchief. H.A. Boyd read the list of presenters, their topics, and gave the enrollment report. The local housing committee gave the messengers their last-minute accommodation assignments.

The third Sunday School Congress took place in Jacksonville, Florida (1908), when the Reverend N.H. Pius and the Reverend Thomas W.J. Tobias of New Orleans led the new song "Hail the Baptist Congress." They dedicated it to the National Baptist Sunday School Congress:

Behold, they come, the National Baptist Congress. See their royal banner, hear their song, See them arching in the glorious quest. Hear them singing as they march-a-long. Hail! Hail! Hail the Baptist Congress! Hail! Hail! Hail, all hail, all Hail, all hail, all Hail the glorious conquest. Go ye out to meet them. Come ye forth and greet them. Join them in their glorious praise, making heavenly arches ring. Come and join them, heavenly arches ring.

Behold the superintendent's leading onward, see the children marching, hear their song; Teachers marching with their royal banner hear them singing as they march along. Hail! Hail! Hail the Baptist Congress! Hail! Hail! Hail, all Hail, all Hail, all Hail, all Hail the glorious conquest! Go ye out to meet them, Come ye forth and greet them. Join them in their glorious praise, making heavenly arches ring. Come and join them, heavenly arches ring.

Behold, See them gathering within the temple, Hearken to their voices how they sing; See each flag unfurled unto the breezes; all join in the chorus as they sing. Hail! Hail! Hail the Baptist Congress! Hail! Hail! Hail, all Hail, all Hail, all Hail, all Hail the glorious conquest. Go ye out to meet them. Come ye forth and greet them. Join them in their glorious praise, making heavenly arches ring. Come and join them, heavenly arches ring.

—T.W.J. Tobias

The Reverend Nathaniel H. Pius was one of the chief characters in turning the annual Congress into a successful Christian musical experience. He was the author of *Outline of Baptist History* (1911), published by the NBPB and designed to be a tool to teach Negro Sunday school students and other Negro Baptists the correct background of Baptist faith. Upon R.H. Boyd's urging, the Reverend Pius became superintendent of the NBPB's teacher training department and editor of the *Metoka* and *Galeda* magazines.

The next four Congress sessions met in Nashville (1909), Atlanta (1910), Meridian, Mississippi (1911), and Birmingham (1912). Henry A. Boyd said, "The Congress, in going to Meridian [June 7-12], will serve more than half of all the membership of our denomination." He urged 25,000 Negro Baptist churches to send representatives, according to the *Nashville Globe* (January 13, 1911). In Birmingham, the parade ended at the 16th Street Baptist Church.

When the 20th century dawned, the National Baptist Convention was attended by an estimated 56 percent of Negro Christians. There were 37,770 Negro churches and 3,685,097 Negro worshipers of all faiths, according to Carter G. Woodson, *The History of the Negro Church* (1927, 1945, p. 261). As Negro Baptists grew in greater numbers, more internal politics, jealousy, and rivalry developed among them. Moreover, upstart Negro denominations were attracting black Baptists in the South. The black community soon would have more preachers than trained school teachers. This development was affecting the denominational convention and the Publishing Board's efforts to educate, train, and unify Negro Baptists.

Rev. Charles Henry Clark ▶

◀ Rev. J. P. Robinson

Boyd Family, 1890s ▶

◀ NBPB Chorus,
Early 1900s

CHAPTER THREE
1906–1922
Maturity, Controversy, Growth, and the End of an Era for the Publishing Board

Some argue that the greatest needs of the Negro race are religion, morality, higher education, industrial education, and wealth. I hold that the Negro needs all of these. But, if he needs one thing more than another, he needs racial confidence, racial fidelity, racial patriotism, and racial love. —*Richard Henry Boyd*

By 1906, the National Baptist Publishing Board had become America's largest Negro publishing firm. Books, booklets, and Sunday school materials constantly flowed from its presses; and the company's reputation in publishing and Baptist missionary work became national and international. The NBPB had sold 10,000 copies of the *National Baptist Hymnal*; and a pocket-size edition was published in 1906, including songs for all religious occasions. Nevertheless, few literary critics give credit to the NBPB for contributing to the Negro Renaissance of 1890-1915.

The Publishing Board soon had an impressive list of books and publications: James H. Eason, *Pulpit and Platform Efforts: Sanctifications vs. Fanaticism* (1899); R.H. Boyd, *Pastor's Guide and Parliamentary Rules* (1900); Allen D. Hurt, *The Beacon Lights of Tennessee Baptists* (1900); *Golden Gems: A Song Book for the Church Choir, the Pew, and the Sunday School* (1901); E.C. Morris, *Sermons, Addresses, and Reminiscences and Important Correspondence* (1901); Lewis G. Jordan, *Up the Ladder in Foreign Missions* (1901); Silas Floyd, *The Life of Charles T. Walker, D.D., the Black Surgeon and Pastor of Mt. Olive Church, New York City* (1902); R.H. Boyd and William Rosborough, *The National Baptist Hymnal* (1903); Jacob T. Brown, *Theological Kernels* (1903); Eugene Carter, *Once a Methodist, Now a Baptist* (1905); and Maurice Corbett, *The Harp of Ethiopia* (1914). The book by Corbett was a militant pronouncement against racial oppression; and one of the book's poems stated, "And blood the means will ever be, by which men gain their liberty. Not blood of someone in their stead. But blood which themselves have shed."

Boyd gave financial support to a newcomer in Nashville, the young Sutton E. Griggs, Jr. (b. 1872). In this way, the NBPB helped Griggs publish his first books, including *Imperium in Imperio: A Study of the Negro Race Problem* (1899) and a number of novels. The 1899 book by Griggs fictionalized a revolution led by educated Negroes in Texas; indeed, one literary critic found works of Sutton Griggs, Jr. to be "fanatical Negro nationalism," according to Robert A. Bone's *The Negro Novel in America* (1965, p. 33). By 1915, Sutton E. Griggs, Jr., unlike his father in Texas, became openly hostile to R.H. Boyd; and before moving to Memphis to pastor another church, Griggs was hostile to many others and openly in dispute with his former church in East Nashville over finances and money used to publish his novels.

The six-building NBPB complex had new printing presses with automatic continuous paper feeders and a capacity of 15,000 impressions per hour. Workers installed a new Michele Press and a book printing press to keep pace with the demand for reading materials. The second floor housed the proofreading department, a new Washington hand press for taking impressions and making banners, and two new linotype machines. On December 28, 1907, the NBPB opened the new chapel and presented a gold-headed cane, engraved "National Baptist Publishing Board, 1896," to Dr. J. M. Frost. Daily plant operations became the responsibility of the assistant secretary, Henry A. Boyd. New Year's 1908 began with the traditional NBPB Annual Dinner, with Boyd offering prayers, the audience singing Christian songs, and the staff laying out the elaborate dinner on the banquet tables in the company's chapel. The employees presented R.H. Boyd with a gold watch in appreciation for his leadership and managerial skills.

At the 1909 National Baptist Convention session in Columbus, Ohio, R.H. Boyd reported that the Home Mission Board had built a church in the Panama Canal Zone and intended to build a school and four more churches with the NBPB's help. The NBPB employed 150 workers and constantly was installing new equipment. The inventory listed $178,429 in machinery, books, periodicals, office equipment, and supplies. The Publishing Board bought the D.E. Dortch Publishing Company's song books, plates, and copyrights, thus gaining control of 4,000 Baptist denomination songs. The NBPB offered courses in child nurture, studies of the Bible, Old and New Testament history, and general Baptist history; students received a diploma upon completion of the courses.

R.H. Boyd complained to the NBC that they should help finance the *National Baptist Union*—or take it over. So they did. The 1909 session authorized a "Union Publishing Committee" to go to Nashville and take control of the *National Baptist Union;* the NBPB began publication of the *National Baptist Review.* Due to a lack of money and expertise, the NBC committee gave up publication of the *National Baptist Union.* Boyd merged the two papers into the weekly *National Baptist Union-Review.*

By 1911-1912, the NBPB was generating $200,000 a year, more than all the other NBC affiliated boards combined. Morris said, "It is generally known the National Baptist Publishing Board had the most phenomenal growth of any of the Boards of our Convention. Yet it has been under constant fire almost all the years of its existence." Morris' mediating remarks, annual audits, and visiting committees did not satisfy Boyd's critics or deal with the preachers' jealousy against the Publishing Board's success. In 1912, the NBPB produced 32 periodicals, and the output of Sunday school materials reached 55.8 million copies. The workers could produce 30,000 to 50,000 magazines per day, yet they still needed newer and faster machines. The field secretary, Beckham, visited every state in the Union, parts of Canada, and Europe to promote the Home Mission Board and the NBPB materials and programs. In cooperation with the Fireside School, Bible conferences were started to endorse the idea of Bible reading in the home. Children's Day programs were promoted in the churches and supported by NBPB materials. In 1912, R.H. Boyd personally visited the Panama Canal Zone to further the Publishing Board's work and the NBC Home Mission Board. He also was a speaker at Roger Williams University in March 1912.

The American Baptist Publication Society began to withdraw from the southern sphere of work in 1912. Yet, A. J. Rowland told the 1912 National Baptist Convention session delegates that the

ABPS continued to use Negro workers in mission work in the South. The Northern and Southern Baptists met at Hot Springs, Arkansas, on January 25, 1912, and agreed to cooperate rather than fight about the Negro Baptists. Henry L. Morehouse of the American Baptist Home Mission Society also spoke at the 1912 NBC session and assured the delegates that the Northern Baptists remained interested and involved in the welfare of Negro Baptists. Richard Henry Boyd urged the convention to give Dr. Morehouse a resolution of thanks and appreciation. Later, the Atlanta Baptist College changed its name to Morehouse College.

Between 1913 and 1915, the NBPB continued to grow and prosper. The National Baptist Convention's 1913 session was held in Nashville, and R.H. Boyd was able to show the delegates firsthand how the NBPB operated its plant and headquarters at 523 2nd Avenue North and Locust Street. The main building on the corner resembled a two-story brick mansion with a copula, ornamentation around the windows, and a picket fence around the complex near the sidewalks. Here, the NBPB would remain until moving to a new facility 60 years later.

The National Baptist Publishing Board experienced a tough year in 1914. At the annual National Baptist Convention session in Philadelphia, President Elias C. Morris said, "There is no reason whatever for any friction between the Convention and its boards...."

The anti-NBPB faction, however, secured a resolution to change the National Baptist Convention's charter, incorporate the organization, and give it control and ownership over the boards that had separate charters. The debate prompted heated exchanges on the floor of the convention. In October 1914, NBPB board members published, *Protest of the National Baptist Publishing Board Against the Acts of the Commission on Incorporation*. They printed a copy of the 1898 Tennessee Charter in the *National Baptist Union-Review* to show that the NBPB was a private, non-profit corporation. Boyd resigned as head of the Home Mission Board, saying "I tendered my resignation for the good of the work...."

Nathaniel H. Pius died on October 28, 1914, after an 11-month illness, leaving a wife and two daughters. The Publishing Board's Brass Band played in the funeral procession from his home at 1817

Scovel Street in Nashville to the First Colored Baptist Church. Pius was a native Texan, a graduate of Leland University, former president of Hearne College, pastor of churches in Texas, Indiana, and Ohio, and former president of Howe Institute (forerunner of today's LeMoyne College) in Memphis, Tennessee, before coming to the Publishing Board in 1908. Richard H. Boyd, then 71 years old, took a break in mid-November 1914. Instead of enjoying a vacation, he visited churches in New Orleans, San Antonio, Austin, and other places. He received big ovations, often with large delegations waiting for his arrival at train stations. Boyd soon faced more disappointing news in December when field secretary Beckham died while on a trip to Missouri. He was taken to the First Colored Baptist Church, where Ellington gave the eulogy. Six days later, December 29, another NBC commission arrived to take over the NBPB; but the commission left in a day or two, proposing a resolution to incorporate the National Baptist Convention at the September 1915 session.

At the 18th annual New Year's dinner at the Publishing Board, the president of Guadalupe College gave the blessing. R.H. Boyd recited the company's history. On April 15, 1915, Indiana Dickson, R.H. Boyd's mother, died in her home at 1602 Heiman Street. His half brothers had arrived in Nashville to sit with their mother during her last days. People remembered Mrs. Dickson as a woman who would direct her son, R.H. Boyd, to send wood and coal fuel to poor families during winters. At the annual Sunday School Congress session, she was admirably called "the mother of the Publishing Board." The NBPB closed the offices in honor of her funeral, before the body was shipped from Nashville to Houston for burial.

When the Southern Baptist Convention held its annual session in Houston in May 1915, R.H. Boyd was acknowledged in the following manner:

> A monument to Negro executive management and skill is the great National Baptist Publishing Board at Nashville, where Dr. R.H. Boyd, a former slave, began as late as 1896 without a penny of capital, but which now covers a half block in the Tennessee capital, and is valued at $365,000. In justice, it should be said Dr. Boyd [depended on] our secretary of the Sunday School Board, Dr. J. M.

Frost, a sympathetic coadjutor, but he was able to stand alone, and now this great institution not only publishes all classes of denominational literature, but furnishes Sunday school requisites and church furniture and binds and prints books after the most modern methods" (*National Baptist Union-Review*, May 15, 1915).

Through the 1950s, Negro communities enjoyed and adored their professional Negro Baseball League teams, and picnics in July and August were favorite gatherings for the Negro people. The 10th Annual Picnic of the NBPB took place on July 31, 1915, at Greenwood Park. The employees of the NBPB played the Greenwood Giants Baseball Team. No one paid attention to the score because the event was pure fun.

During September 7-8, 1915, the NBC session convened in Chicago's Regimental Armory on 16th and Michigan, where the incorporation controversy caused a denominational split. Those recognizing the Publishing Board's autonomy formed the National Baptist Convention of America, Unincorporated (NBCA); and those on the other side became the National Baptist Convention, USA, Inc. The latter persuaded some Nashville preachers to file a suit in the Tennessee courts on September 30, 1915, in order to gain control of the NBPB; but they lost the case during the next four years. The National Baptist Convention of America printed its materials through the NBPB. An advisory board of NBCA members monitored the doctrine and policy of all Baptist publications furnished them by the National Baptist Publishing Board to their churches and Sunday schools. The NBPB continued to publish the *Union-Review*, with J. H. Frank as editor. "The year 1915, then, was truly the end of the beginning of a new era for black Baptists," said Owen D. Pelt and R. L. Smith in *The Story of the National Baptists* (1961).

The 1916 session of the National Baptist Convention of America met in Kansas City, Missouri, on September 6-11 under President Edward P. Jones. Georgia DeBaptiste became head of the Women's Auxiliary of the NBCA, which convened in Kansas City also on September 6-11, 1916. Harriet Albertine Boyd served as chairperson of the women's program committee. After James M. Frost died in 1916, relations between the National Baptist Publishing Board and the Southern Baptist Convention cooled.

In April 1917, when America officially entered the First World War, the NBPB supported the nation's effort. The 37th session of the NBCA convened in Atlanta on September 5-11, 1917. Approximately 1,587 delegates attended the session, including the Women's Auxiliary Convention that met at Liberty Baptist Church. Georgia DeBaptiste-Ashburn said, "Our convention is placed in our hands by the providence of God, but it is placed in our hands, and we must all feel the responsibility resting upon our own shoulders." The Missionary Baptist General Convention of Texas sent large delegations to the NBCA session and the NBPB Sunday School Congress session. The National Baptist Chorus sang a moving rendition of "Soon-a-Will Be Done with the Troubles of the World." A Southern Baptist Convention representative spoke at the session, urging NBCA reconciliation with the NBC, USA. Richard Henry Boyd sponsored the resolution. Later that evening, R.H. Boyd presented the NBPB's 1917 report to the convention, saying, "We make everything from a post card to an encyclopedia and from a calling card to a Bible. Our literature is written by Negroes, set upon linotype machines owned and operated by Negroes, printed on printing presses owned and operated by Negroes, finished in a book binding plant owned and operated by Negroes, and sent out for use by Negro Baptists." The NBPB printed 7,266,270 pieces of literature, compared to 6,750,063 in 1916. The Publishing Board published 25 books, various booklets, an eight-page weekly *Union-Review*, pamphlets, and the *Sunday School Commentary*. Boyd reminded the delegates the NBPB's "real work began in San Antonio, Texas in 1895. We have been able to hold our own despite massive negative publicity in newspapers, circulars, pulpits, and pamphlets throughout the country."

The National Baptist Publishing Board officials bought a new duplex Webb perfecting printing press that could print on both sides of the paper, paste, fold, trim, and deliver a multipage newspaper at the rate of 3,700 copies per hour. This was the first machine of its kind to be installed in Nashville. The National Baptist Convention of America met in September in Norfolk, Virginia, where the delegates launched a $2 million endowment fund campaign to support aged and retired Negro Baptist ministers. Few Negro churches had ministers on full-time salaries; but they often augmented the pastor's meager income with a "Rush Party," which involved mostly the women of the church. These ladies gathered supplies of food and some financial donations and rushed over to the preacher's house to surprise him and his family.

In 1920, when the National Baptist Convention of America (NBCA) met in Columbus, Ohio, the NBPB reported an increase in current publications, as well as the launch of new ones, including the *Baptist Church Directory, National Gospel Voices, National Anthem Series,* and *Celestial Showers*—all in hard covers. The Publishing Board had $231,486 in revenues for 1920. During the winter, Boyd visited the churches in the Panama Canal Zone. He was considering retirement. The gentleman was only a couple years shy of 80. On the last night of the NBCA session, Boyd became quite ill. He recovered and later went on speaking engagements to 35 churches and the Florida Progressive Baptist Convention. He continued to direct the daily operations of the NBPB until Henry Allen returned from overseas after attending an international Sunday school meeting.

Charles H. Clark accepted a lucrative offer to pastor the Ebenezer Baptist Church in Chicago in 1920. The Reverend John R. Ridley replaced him at Nashville's Mt. Olive Baptist Church, and the Reverend G.B. Taylor of Nashville replaced Ridley as chairman of the Publishing Board. Taylor was a native Texan, pastor of Lake Providence Baptist Church in Nashville, chairman of the Colored YMCA board, and head of the Stones River Baptist District Association.

In order to better educate Sunday school personnel, the NBPB already had begun publishing the annual *Sunday School Lesson Commentary,* which contained scriptures and true Baptist tenets. The Congress department encouraged Negro Baptists to study the Bible based on the *International Sunday School Lesson* plan. The quarterlies, which included elementary, intermediary, and advanced lessons along with picture cards, helped churches to teach congregations diversified by age, gender, and degrees of literacy. *The National Baptist Hymnal* (1903), including a pocket-size edition (1906), provided songs for all church functions. The hymnal contained many tunes that kept the Negro Baptists grounded in the history of their faith, including old slave spirituals. Boyd's *Baptist Pastor's Guide and*

Parliamentary Rules (1900) gave additional help in preserving order in the Negro Baptist churches.

The National Baptist Publishing Board had become America's largest Negro publishing house, and this necessitated the division of the early Sunday School Congress into Sunday school work, Baptist Young People's Training Union work, and special features including sessions for preachers, church officers, and preachers' wives. The Boyd family, NBPB officers, leaders of the convention, and officers of the various boards often arrived in the host city on Sunday and held services that evening at the host church. After the Tuesday morning parade, the Congress began on Tuesday evening with a concert arranged by the host church that drew local church members and delegates dressed in their finest clothes. Working sessions began in earnest on Wednesday morning and ended on Friday evening. The format consisted of departmental meetings, singing, instructive readings, and lectures. The latter frequently was used because of the low rate of literacy among Negroes; only a generation had elapsed since slavery had ended. The Publishing Board advertised its publications, services, and products, and, gradually, other religious vendors were attracted to the huge sessions.

Besides competing against the new denominations that were sweeping up young Baptists in "the Black Belt" of the South, the objective of the Sunday School Congress was to create a more healthy sentiment among the Baptist Churches in regard to the Sunday Church School movement and the Baptist Young People's Union movement. The BYPU related to Baptist doctrine, spirit, history, and other elements of the Baptist church. The activities and programs were based on Proverbs 22:6: "Train up a child in the way he should go: and when he is old, he will not depart from it" (KJV). The Publishing Board also wanted to promote a systematic study of the Bible from the International Sunday School Lesson perspective.

Other featured events of the Congress consisted of the Congress Parade and Metoka and Galeda Night, both of which prominently featured children and young adults. The Metoka and Galeda Department had been organized by R.H. Boyd after hearing Negroes complain about the National Baracca and Philathea meetings, where colored people felt unwelcome. Boyd said: "If we cannot be welcomed in a religious and fraternal way, then we will make our own department." He previously had asked the late Reverend Pius to find two words in the dead languages—which turned out to be "Metok" and "Galed"—to use for the new department. Around 1911, Tobias wrote the theme song "On, On, Metokas and Galedas." The model Sunday school was sponsored by the host church, and a messenger was asked to take charge of the school for the day. This practice continued to be followed, according to the *Union-Review* (February 16, 1946). These aspects of the Sunday School Congress would become the Mini-Congress for the youth. Certificates and credits were issued in later years and expanded in 1981 under the direction of T .B. Boyd III. There were sessions for the education and training of ministers and their wives to help them perform better in the increasingly complex Baptist ministry.

The operations of the NBPB and the Sunday School Congress grew by leaps and bounds. Every September, R.H. Boyd had to assure the denominational convention the Congress was not a policy-making body or competitor meant to overshadow convention programs. Boyd told the NBC delegates the Sunday School Congress was "the greatest adjunct or the greatest assistance or agency our [National Baptist] Publishing Board has to increase the circulation of periodicals and other Sunday school requisites." On June 14-18, 1916, the Congress met in Vicksburg, Mississippi, to which 22 states had sent representatives, pastors, Sunday school superintendents, and children. By then, the National Baptist Publishing Board and the National Baptist Sunday School Congress were affiliated with the National Baptist Convention of America.

The 11th session of the Sunday School Congress was held in Nashville on June 13-18, 1917. NBCA and the NBPB planned the event. Prior to the event, in April, Richard and Henry Boyd and others attended a great "Sunday school mass meeting" hosted by churches in Springfield, Tennessee. Henry Allen was expecting 300 voices and choirs from 35 churches to comprise the National Baptist Congress Choir. H. B. P. Johnson of Muskogee, Oklahoma, arrived on May 27 in Nashville to start the choir rehearsals at Mt. Olive Baptist Church.

One older church member recalled Congress was commenced with "Hail the Baptist Congress" and "Onward Christian Soldiers." The sessions were scheduled at Mt. Olive and other local churches, including Pleasant Green, St. John, Jefferson Street, Mt. Zion, St. John AME, and St. Andrew's Presbyterian. Meetings were also held in the chapel of the Publishing Board on 2nd Avenue North. About 5,000 persons participated in the parade to the mass meeting, which was held in downtown Nashville's Ryman Auditorium where 7,000 attended. The Congress Band performed at Greenwood Park's beautiful bandstand. R.H. Boyd, who some called "the great oak in the forest of the Baptists," made a few remarks. Private cars and electric streetcars transported the messengers from place to place. The messengers represented 35 states. Alabama and Tennessee had the largest number of delegates according to the *Globe* (June 22, 1917).

The 1917 Sunday Congress was especially inclusive of the youth. "The Racial Influence of the Negro Doll Club" and "How to Get and Hold the 'Teen Age' Pupils in the Sunday School" were among the 12 topics of the Sunday Congress. The Metoka and Galeda clubs held their huge banquet at the Colored YMCA, downtown on 4th Avenue. The Fourth Annual A.F. Boy Cadets, under W. H. Crawford, conducted drills and practices on the Fisk University Campus on 18th Avenue North. The "Exhibits and Paraphernalia" section was displayed in the NBPB's headquarters and plant on 2nd Avenue North. Louretha V. Chambers, editor of the *Metoka* and *Galeda* magazines, planned the children's classes. A Cadet Band of 14-year old boys furnished the music, and the Rising Star Glee Club of Shreveport, Louisiana, held daily concerts in cooperation with the Congress Choir.

The start of the Boy Cadets, drill teams, and Cadet Band were reflections of efforts by the Negro Baptists to address the issues of juvenile delinquency at the turn of the 20th century. When Negroes increased their urban population percentages, the social problems that accompanied urbanization seemed to multiply. After America entered the First World War (1917-1919), the idea of drill exercises among the Boy Cadets and Girls' Doll Clubs took hold, merging the concepts of a just war with religion and youth discipline. In the *Nashville Globe* (May 25, 1917), Henry Allen Boyd said, "We are loyal to the Stars and Stripes, and we mean to stand by the Constitution and the Flag, and at the same time carry the banner of King Emmanuel to every dark corner of this great country." Nearly a half million Negroes would serve in American units at home and in Europe, including dozens who won the French Medal of Honor (Croix de Guerre).

The late W. H. Crawford and J. C. Lott of Austin, Texas, organized the Cadets. Richard Henry and Henry Allen Boyd made the Cadets a department of the Congress and published the *Cadets Manual on Drill and Tactics* (1918). Several black colleges had military training corps on campus by 1919-1921. The National Baptist Publishing Board, the Sunday School Congress, and the National Baptist Convention of America all supported the nation's war effort. They reflected this by instilling military and Christian discipline in young Negro Baptists who "Marched for Jesus." Perhaps these efforts diminished President Woodrow Wilson's threat to censor Negro newspapers criticizing the "war abroad to save Democracy," even though there was no war at home to save Democracy from Jim Crow. The Negroes knew the difference but took a non-confrontational approach in order to further their civil rights goals.

The Sunday School Congress and Teachers Training became one of the NBPB's largest divisions, with departments for Bible conferences, primary teachers, intermediate teachers, advanced teachers, Metoka and Galeda classes, Boy Cadets, Negro Doll Clubs, missionaries, Baptist Young People's Union, home classes, and sociology and applied science classes. To the members of the NBCA, the Reverend Boyd said, "Our Sunday School Congress is not held for raising money. To the contrary, our NBPB spends money to make this Congress what it is." Messengers and delegates toured the nearby NBPB facilities and modern plant. "There are no visitors. All are welcome, all find something to do, and everyone is heard [at the Sunday School Congress]," said Boyd, according to the *Globe* (April 27, 1917).

The annual session of the Sunday School Congress met in Bessemer, Alabama on June 11, 1919. Huge crowds waited for the arrival of the "Congress Special" train. The Reverend W. H. Wood, president of the General Baptist Sunday School Convention of Alabama, sponsored the session. The NBPB's 36-voice Choral Society and the Congress Band performed. Twenty-six states sent representatives to the next Sunday School Congress. Attendees could get a train ticket from Nashville to attend the session which was more than two weeks' pay for many of them, but they saved money all year just to be there. Congress Secretary Henry A. Boyd explained: "The aim of the Sunday School Congress is to build front line Sunday schools, to advance modern Sunday school methods, foster Sunday school mission, and help on the plan of child evangelism."

The National Boy Cadets were among the first to arrive at the 1919 Sunday School Congress in Bessemer, Alabama. They were dressed in replica World War I military uniforms and used the new book of tactics and bugle calls. They were supported by the 14-piece Congress Band. C. H. Clark, chairman of the NBPB, J. P. Robinson, chairman of the Home Mission Board, and Edward P. Jones, president of the NBCA, stood together for photographs. J.L. Harding, a NBPB member and president of the Negro Baptist Association of Tennessee, along with other NBPB members (G. B. Taylor, Clark, Robinson, J. C. Fielder, L. L. Campbell, R.H. Boyd, and H. A. Boyd) also graced the scene, according to the *Union-Review* (April 19, June 8, 14, 1919).

The June 16, 1920, Congress session was held in Springfield, Illinois, the home of former President Abraham Lincoln, "the Great Emancipator." In that day and time, Boyd and almost all other Negro voters were loyal to the Republican Party, as they had been since 1867. Delegates visited Lincoln's grave and Sunday School Congress, and NBPB officials laid a wreath on the site. The Congress Band played "America." The sessions were held in the Springfield High School and the City Armory because no church was large enough to hold the Congress by then. The "March for Jesus" parade traveled around the State Capitol before entering the meeting hall. The Springfield Race Riot of August 1908 had embarrassed the nation and led white and Negro liberals and civil rights activists to meet in 1909 to form the NAACP. At the 1920 Sunday School Congress, it was announced that Henry A. Boyd would represent the Publishing Board at the World Sunday School Congress in Tokyo, Japan. His daughter, Katherine, accompanied him to Japan. Delegates donated funds to help with the trip as they sang a soulful rendition of "God Be With You Until We Meet Again."

The Sunday School Congress continued to grow during the next 16 years. However, many records for these years were lost due to a fire, expansions, and renovations of the Publishing Board's headquarters. The preparations for Boyd's annual Sunday School Congress eventually engaged several committees in the host city. The committees' names and responsibilities were as follows: (1) The Music Committee planned and presented the pre-Congress musical for the night preceding the official opening of the Congress. This committee also was responsible for the music during the General Assembly and any special musical events; (2) The Souvenir Book Committee solicited advertisements and distributed booklets, including the Congress schedule in order to financially support the host's expenses; (3) The Hospitality Committee prepared the welcome and amenities for the messengers, including welcome signs, greeters, courtesy cars, souvenir packets, information about the city and local attractions, and other information; (4) The Host Finance Committee consisted of various cooperating churches or members and accounted for incoming funds, deposits, disbursements, and a financial report at the end of the Congress; (5) The Transportation Committee provided courtesy cars for the messengers to make the trips between their accommodations and the central meeting place; (6) The Publicity Committee promoted the Congress and its activities among local churches and the wider host city; and (7) The Host Pastor Committee embodied the Steering Committee, which preceded the Congress by 18 months, establishing the other committees and working with local pastors, churches, and city agencies to ensure a smooth, successful Congress. By 1921-1922, the National Baptist Publishing Board printed 15 periodicals, including three weeklies, two monthlies, and 10 quarterlies. Due to the economic depression of 1921, revenues were down. The expenses were up, and the Board suffered a $7,000 deficit.

Tragedy occurred in 1922. On April 6, Richard H. Boyd's son, J. Blaine, died, and the health of the 79-year-old Richard Boyd continued to deteriorate. On May 31, his condition worsened and physician W.R. Baker of Cedar Street came to the house at 1602 Heiman Street and began treating him. There was not much that could be done because diabetes, old age, and long years of work as a slave and freedman were taking away his life. The Reverend Richard Henry Boyd passed on August 23, 1922, at 8:30 a.m. The funeral was scheduled for August 28; but the NBCA, which was scheduled to meet September 6-11, 1922, changed its meeting place from Denver, Colorado to Nashville in order to attend the funeral and pay homage to the fallen leader. On Saturday morning, his body was buried in Nashville's Greenwood Cemetery on Elm Hill Pike, with Preston Taylor and Company Undertakers handling the arrangements (Davidson County, Death Certificate No. 300). Three thousand NBCA delegates packed Nashville's downtown Ryman Auditorium, according to the *Nashville Banner* (September 6, 1922). The president of the NBCA said, "No man could tell of the tears and sorrows in accomplishing that willingness as the venerable, earnest, and conscientious Dr. R.H. Boyd." The Reverend Elias C. Morris, president of the National Baptist Convention, passed on September 9, 1922 and was interred in his hometown of Helena, Arkansas. The death of the two Baptist leaders signaled the end of an era for the Negro Baptists.

W. L. Cansler (member of the founding "printing committee" of November 1896) and E. W. D. Isaac witnessed Boyd's last will and testament. The document left the bulk of Boyd's estate to his wife and the rest to his children "to share and share alike." The will was probated on December 22, 1922, according to Davidson County, Will Book No. 4, 1922-1924. There was no great pile of wealth left behind, as dissidents in the National Baptist Convention, USA, Inc. had claimed, according to Davidson County Deed Books. Boyd's family had lived at 523 Market (2nd) Street for years before they could afford to build a house at 1602 Heiman Street in North Nashville just two blocks north of Fisk University, according to *Nashville City Directory, 1907*. Richard H. Boyd had been a member of the Colored YMCA advisory board, Tennessee Interracial League, Knights of Phythias, the Masons, board of directors of the International Sunday School Association, and president of Citizens Bank. He also was a member of the U.B.F. Society and Odd Fellows. He was a Renaissance man who was ahead of his peers. Edward P. Jones poetically spoke of the Reverend Richard Henry Boyd:

> Upon [his] brow have fallen needless criticisms, charges and countercharges, unwarranted by facts, but in the main ignorantly alleged and for reasons personally sinister, advanced and maintained. But, so clean had he washed his hands from the seductive

influences of passion and hate that his immortal documents shall grow white in purpose with the years.

The NBPB and friends established the Richard H. Boyd Memorial Commission to complete a bronze statue in his likeness and honor his birthday each year. The statue continues to grace the entrance to the Publishing Board. Richard H. Boyd Week is celebrated in the company's chapel every March. Boyd's Normal and Industrial Institute in Oakwood, Texas was named in his honor. Decades later, young black businesspersons and aspiring entrepreneurs would see Richard Henry Boyd as an exemplary entrepreneur, businessman, and civic leader; they would name the Nashville-Middle Tennessee annual Minority Enterprise Development Week in his honor. Thus, long after his death Richard Henry Boyd (1843-1922) still sets an example for others to follow in uplifting themselves and other people.

◀ Baptist Ministers Alliance

Mrs. L.P. Benham ▶

◀ Old NBPB Plant and
Headquarters, 1910

Dr. C.J.W. Boyd ▶

H.A. Boyd Band ▶

◀ Mrs. H.A. Boyd

Mrs. R.H. Boyd ▶

◀ R.H. Boyd

◀ R.H. Boyd Memorial Building

R.H. Thorburne "Our Missionary in Panama" ▶

◀ Bessie Thorburne, NBPB's Missionary to Panama

R.H. Boyd, President ▶

▲ H.A. Boyd and R.H. Boyd

▲ Rev. S.N. Vass

Col. W.S. Bradden, D.D. ▶

◀ Rev. W.W. Brown

Miss N.H. Burroughs ▶

Rev. E.C. Morris ▶

▲ Rev. H. J. Moses

Mt. Olive B.C.
Usher Board ▶

◀ Mrs. Jenie B. Paul Murphy

◀ National Baptist Revised Hymnal

National Jubilee Melodies ▼

◀ National Baptist Banner

Founders and Directors of One Cent Savings Bank and Trust Company, Nashville, 1904 ▼

CHAPTER FOUR

R.H. Boyd: Entrepreneur, Business Manager, and Leader

The 20th century will prove that he who steers the wheels of commerce will direct and control the civilized world. —Richard Henry Boyd

While building the National Baptist Publishing Board, Richard H. Boyd and the management added other programs, companies, and enterprises. To be sure, these activities illustrated the multifaceted life of this Renaissance man, the wider legacy left by R.H. Boyd, and his enduring influence on black Christians and other African-American citizens.

Richard H. Boyd and others formed the Union Transportation Company as a result of the local boycott against Tennessee's March 1905 Jim Crow streetcar law. Boyd and his colleagues bought some steam and electric-powered six-passenger cars and started a Negro streetcar line. There were three routes across the city, charging five cent fares. The company was forced to close in 1907 after the city imposed a tax on the cars. Boyd, Preston Taylor, and other officers and stockholders (mostly women) voted to sell the electric cars to the Jamestown Exposition in Virginia.

In order to publicize the boycott, Boyd and his colleagues started the *Nashville Globe*, a weekly newspaper, on January 14, 1906. Frank O. Battle edited the paper until his death in 1910, and Henry Allen Boyd became the editor until his death in 1959. R.H. Boyd, H. A. Boyd, and other NBPB employees chartered the Globe Publishing Company to separate the newspaper from the nonprofit NBPB. Dock A. Hart, the chief NBPB printer, managed the Globe Publishing Company. "The *Globe* came into existence as a much needed weapon of defense, a champion of its people's rights," stated the Nashville *Globe* (January 8, 1911), which ceased publication in 1960.

R.H. Boyd and colleagues formed the National Baptist Church Supply Company, which began installing built-in pipe organs in churches in 1902. Boyd got the National Baptist Church Supply Company started by using his personal funds to buy a bankrupt company. A vacant lot owned by the NBPB was used in return for turning the Church Supply Company building over to the NBPB within ten years. The company built, sold, and shipped church furniture and supplies until it could no longer do so due to stiff competition by better financed companies.

R.H. Boyd formed the National Negro Doll Company around 1905. His son, Henry Allen, managed the Doll Company. The *Globe's* advertisement proclaimed the following:

> These dolls are not made of that disgraceful and humiliating type that we have grown accustomed to seeing Negro dolls made of. They represent the intelligent and refined Negro of the day, rather than the type of toy that is usually given to the children and, as a rule, used as a scarecrow.

Boyd ordered batches of dolls from Germany, formed Negro Dolls Clubs, and persuaded the Baptist convention to endorse the idea. He wanted to instill confidence, ability, and integrity in his people; and he believed the place to start was giving a positive self-image to the children.

Richard and Henry Allen Boyd helped lead the Tennessee Agricultural and Industrial State Normal School Association (1909), which successfully lobbied state officials for placement of the new school (today's Tennessee State University, 1912-present) in Nashville, Davidson County. The two men also were important leaders in the Nashville Negro Board of Trade, which persuaded the city to build a new Pearl High School for Negroes in 1916.

Richard Henry Boyd, the NBPB, and the NBCA established the National Baptist Theological Seminary and Training School. Boyd persuaded the National Baptist Convention of America (NBCA) to buy the abandoned Boscobel College campus for white girls in East

Nashville. The campus included two main brick buildings on ten acres of land overlooking the Cumberland River, sixty-five dormitory rooms with bathrooms between every two rooms, steam heat and ventilation, a large recreation room, a chapel, eight classrooms with fine desks, five offices, and a dining hall for hundreds, the *Nashville Globe* reported (June 22, 1917). The school opened its doors on June 28, 1918. At the September 10-18, 1930, NBCA session, a committee recommended selling the Boscobel campus to "throw all [their] educational strength to [their] great school in Virginia" (Virginia Union Seminary). Critics said the local seminary could not survive under the shadows of "towering colleges [Tennessee State and Fisk] as are in Nashville," and closed in 1934.

R.H. Boyd was a lifelong Republican but never ran for public office. His colleague, lawyer, and banker, James C. Napier, was head of the local Republican Party, a member of the Republican State Executive Committee, and delegate to the National Republican Convention. When white Republicans tried to oust Napier from the state committee, Boyd wrote a letter to Negro churches, urging them to stand up and let their political power be felt. He said, (March 10, 1900): "I fear a destruction of our political rights as a race in this state. You are aware of the fact that there seems to be concert of action in every Southern state to disfranchise the Negroes at the ballot box." At the Davidson County Republican meeting, Boyd and his Negro colleagues insisted Napier be one of the Tennessee delegates sent to the National Republican Convention. Boyd and Henry Allen used the *Globe* to galvanize Negro voters. When President W. Howard Taft (R) appointed Napier as Register of the U.S. Treasury (1911-1913), R.H. Boyd proudly said, "Mr. Napier is my personal friend and has been my lawyer during all of my business and professional life. He is a Negro of whom the whole race is proud." Henry Allen assumed the leadership of the Davidson County Lincoln-Douglass Negro Republican Club in Nashville-Davidson County.

After forming the Nashville Chapter of Booker T. Washington's National Negro Business League (NNBL) in 1902, Richard H. Boyd, Napier, and other colleagues formed the One Cent Savings Bank and Trust Company at the November 5, 1903 meeting in Napier's law office. One Cent Bank opened for business in the Napier

Building on January 16, 1904, with $1,600 in capital and $6,500 in deposits. Boyd served as president, Preston Taylor as chairman of the board of directors, and Napier as cashier (manager). The bank made $2,462 profit in 1906, survived the 1907 economic panic, and balanced its books with $43,908 in that year. Richard Boyd said, "It should be clearly understood by the stockholders that this institution was born out of real necessity. It was not organized as a loan company, an investment company, an industrial insurance company, or a pawn shop." In 1920, the One Cent Bank changed its name to Citizens Savings Bank and Trust Company; by 2004, it was America's oldest functioning black-operated bank.

Richard H. Boyd was a civic and religious leader. He served on the Federation Council of Churches in America, Special Committee on the Peace and Arbitration related to the 100th Anniversary Celebration of the Treaty of Ghent, in July 1913. Boyd, a former slave, served as speaker for many Emancipation Proclamation Day programs across America. He joined the crusade to promote land and homeownership among Negroes because only 25 percent of Negro farmers in Tennessee owned their land; and in Nashville, only 28 percent of Negroes owned their homes. Boyd and his son, Henry Allen, along with their colleagues, led the movement to reestablish the Colored YMCA and purchase its own four-story building in downtown Nashville in 1917 at a time when Jim Crow laws denied Negroes the privilege of staying at local YMCA establishments. Boyd insisted the Publishing Board support the nation's World War I effort (1917-1918), even loaning the company's truck to transport Bibles and gifts to downtown railroad stations, where packages were delivered to departing Negro soldiers. Boyd's son, Henry Allen, followed Negro soldiers to their camps, taking photographs, collecting letters, and publishing them in the *Globe*. The NBPB, the Boyd family, and the One Cent Bank invested thousands of dollars in American war bonds.

Lastly, Richard H. Boyd was a leader in civil rights activities. He and the NBPB published *The Separate or 'Jim Crow' Car Laws*, or *Legislative Enactments of Fourteen Southern States* (1907). Boyd said, "The purpose of this little book is to be a constant companion in the pocket or hand of every self-respecting, law-abiding Negro who is compelled to travel by rail in any of the fourteen states of the Union that have passed separate or 'Jim Crow' car laws for the purpose of humiliating and degrading the Negro race in the eyes of all the civilized world."

At the September 4-9, 1929, NBCA session in Norfolk, Virginia, the National Baptist Convention of America's president asked: "What would be the standing and progress of Negroes in America today had there been no Richard Henry Boyd? I am no hero worshiper, but Richard H. Boyd wrought a work in the religious world that shall lend inspiration to the ambitious youth of the land and enrich Baptist history throughout succeeding generations."

◀ James C. Napier, Manager of One Cent Savings Bank

J.W. Bostic ▶

Chicago Ministers & Deacons Alliance ▼

Church Record Roll and Minute Book ▶

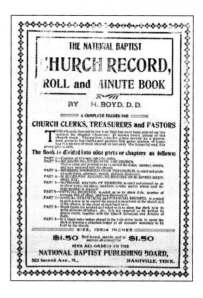

▲ Citizens Savings Bank President's Dinner

▲ Citizens Savings Bank President's Dinner

Citizens Bank & Trust Co. ▶

◀ Mrs. O.W. Coleman

▼ Congress Secretaries & Officials Parade

◀ Congress Band

Congress Entertainment
Committee ▶

CHAPTER FIVE

1922–1959
Henry Allen Boyd, 37 Years at the Helm of the NBPB

Because the National Baptist Publishing Board is operating for the sole purpose of giving service to the race and denomination, every phase of religious life has been considered. The interest of the institution is naturally centered on the things pertaining to religion and spirituality, and that interest is deep and abiding. 'Service' is the keynote of the institution. —Henry Allen Boyd

Henry Allen Boyd (1876-1959) was born on April 15 in Grimes County, Texas. Upon the death of his father, R.H. Boyd, in 1922, he became head of the National Baptist Publishing Board. He also succeeded his father as president of Citizens Savings Bank and Trust Company. Henry A. Boyd attended public schools in his native Palestine, Texas before joining the West Union Baptist Church, headed by his father. Henry Allen also became the first Negro postal agent in San Antonio. Around 1895, he married Lula M. Smith and had one child, Katherine, but Lula passed away. After moving to Nashville to help his father at the NBPB in 1908, Henry Allen Boyd married Georgia Bradford (d. 1952).

Henry Allen Boyd became a director for the Supreme Life Insurance Company, head of the Sunday School Congress, member of the National Council of Churches in Christ in the U.S.A., a board member at Fisk University and Meharry Medical College, and head of the local Negro Republican Club. As an educational leader, he was noted for his role in founding Tennessee A&I State College and as adviser to the president of the institution. Boyd also was editor of the *Nashville Globe* from 1910 until his death. He helped direct the National Baptist Church Supply Company, managed the National Negro Doll Company, and headed the Lincoln-Douglass Voters'

League, a Republican Party club. In the late 1950s, he created a "Weekly Round-Up" in the *Globe* to alert readers about the growing Civil Rights Movement.

H.A. Boyd wasted no time in building and expanding the enterprises left by his father. He signed a joint agreement with the Lott Carey Baptist Foreign Mission Convention in 1925 to do foreign mission work and service Negro Baptist churches in the Eastern United States. He also decided to continue some of the NBPB's traditions: Annual New Year's Day Banquet, prayers and church services in the company's chapel, and the Annual Picnic at Greenwood Park. The latter event usually took place in mid-July, about a month after the completion of the Annual Sunday School Congress.

Henry Allen also added some traditions of his own, including chartered streetcars for the picnic, an Annual Christmas Party, a half day off for Christmas Eve, and a full day for Christmas. He provided a cash bonus in an envelope for employees at Christmas; and he instituted the "President's Dinner" to invite customers of Citizens Bank to dine and discuss concerns. The dinner usually was held in the Colored YMCA where Boyd served as one of the leading directors and founding organizers.

Henry Allen Boyd was a persistent traveler, taking trains from one part of the country to another, speaking at churches, and strengthening the NBPB's ties with district and state Baptist conventions. Word quickly spread when he came into each town because he dressed in fine suits and praised the local Baptists. Henry Allen Boyd constantly was on the road (using trains rather than airplanes) trying to reach as many Negro Christians and pastors as possible. Carter G. Woodson, *The History of the Negro Church* (1927, 1945) estimated 5.6 million Negro church members; 42,585 Negro churches; and 24,560 Negro clergy in the 1920s (p. 290).

When the number of black churches grew, the business of the National Baptist Publishing Board also expanded. At the September 8, 1926, National Baptist Convention of America (NBCA) session, President J.C. Wood said:

> The NBPB will never die as long as Henry Allen Boyd races the country from the Lakes to the Gulf and from the Atlantic to the Pacific, and sings the songs of progress and efficiency. The world's

record will show that those who would criticize and find fault with our NBPB, not one of them have built a worthy institution of any kind.

At the September 1927 NBCA session, Wood said:

And there she stands, the Gibraltar of Baptist thought and teaching and contribution in self-help, freedom, and independence. She has weathered the storms of a thousand seas, withstood the shot and shell of the most bitter adversaries, and she comes into the safe harbor of glorious achievements with sails unfurled and flippant in the breeze; her bosom laden with good things: faith, hope, love, and goodwill toward all men.

Despite the Great Depression of 1929, Citizens Bank survived a rash of bankruptcies in the city; whereas, another black institution, People's Bank, closed. Several banks owned by whites in Nashville also went bankrupt, while the Publishing Board continued to prosper and realize an increase of $24,779 in business.

By 1930, the NBPB had developed an extensive catalog of materials and books for churches; the list of song books included 21 titles. The NBPB carried a large stock of mission supplies, Bibles, collection plates, communion ware, marriage and other certificates, Sunday school material, Baptist Young People's Union supplies, record books, and roll books. To attract the new generation of ministers and church workers, the NBPB began a series of correspondence courses including biblical introduction, exegesis, homiletics, and systematic theology. Boyd said,

Because the National Baptist Publishing is operating for the sole purpose of giving service to our race and denomination, every phase of religious life has been considered. The interest of the institution naturally is centered on the things pertaining to religion and spirit.

The 1930 Sunday School Congress met in Chicago's Ebenezer Baptist Church at 45th and Vincennes Street during June 11-16. Here, Henry Allen Boyd claimed a biblical reason for the existence of the Sunday School Congress. He said, "It was in the month of June, some 1,900 years ago, when the Holy Spirit filled the Upper Room and also filled the waiting disciples who praised God until multitudes came to see and hear" (*Union-Review*, February 22, 1930).

Henry A. Boyd had traveled to Chicago in January to meet with the church's pastor, Charles Henry Clark. They made the preparations with local churches and reserved the Vincennes Hotel, a seven-story brick building, as Congress' headquarters. The Illinois Baptist Association was one of the chief hosts, and a 500-voice choir entertained the audience. The *Union-Review* (March 11, 1930) called for 1,000 boys, ages 6 to 15, to participate in the National Encampment at the National Sunday School and B.Y.P.U. Congress in Chicago. The Reverend S.S. Jones, pastor of Friendship Baptist Church in Chicago, served as Major-General of the Boy Cadet and Camp Fire Girls section.

The parade was held on Sunday afternoon; and despite the Great Depression, 32 states sent 5,000 messengers and visitors. The dignitaries on the pulpit included the National Baptist Theological and Training Seminary trustees: E.R. Carter (pastor of Friendship Baptist Church, Atlanta, Georgia), A.A. Lucas (Texas), J.W. Pitt (Nashville), and J.P. Robinson (Arkansas). J.W. Hurse, the president of the National Baptist Convention of America, was lauded for his 50th anniversary as a pastor. J.P. Robinson, pastor of First Baptist Church in Little Rock since 1890, chair of the NBPB, president of the Progressive Baptist State Convention of Arkansas, editor of the *People's Defender*, chaired the Congress. Carter directed the ministers' conference at the Sunday School Congress. It was announced the NBCA's 15th anniversary session was scheduled to take place in New York City for September 10-15, 1931.

The base of business for the Publishing Board was constantly expanding. By 1934, the company serviced 20,000 Sunday schools and 8,000 churches. In this regard, Henry Allen was a masterful public relations man. He was able to build good relations with the affiliate NBCA, and he used the *Globe* and the *Union-Review* to spread good news about the NBPB. Henry Allen Boyd stated:

It is the nature of a labor of love, because we are all committed to the task of carrying on every phase of this activity so that it will reflect credit upon the [Baptist] denomination, because the institution known as the National Baptist Publishing Board's plant is a wonder of our great denominational structure. I am conscious of the fact that it is, so to speak, the apple of the eye of millions of religious workers who make up the constituency of this body of Missionary Baptists. It is also the pride of people who are not Baptists, because they look upon it as a race institution. The founder and builder, the late Richard H. Boyd, saw it in this way, because he, too, had but one aim in view, and that was to do something worthwhile, something that would stand, something that would be monumental not only in its effort to do good, but that would be lasting, so that this, as well as unborn generations, might look upon it as an institution, a business concern, a religious plant as an expression of what we can do in our day and generations as constructive builders, organizers and operators of a plant that is known throughout the world today.

Many said the 1937 Sunday School Congress was the best ever. Henry Allen was overjoyed with its success, and he invited the delegates to stop in Nashville on the way home from Cincinnati. He entertained a crowd of about 120 in the gymnasium of the Colored YMCA and served a breakfast of fruit cocktail, broiled chicken, hot rolls, hominy grits, croquets, rice, bacon, eggs, apple rings, and coffee. Boyd then took the guests on a tour of the nearby NBPB. They visited the local Baptist seminary; the 20-acre Greenwood Park; the campuses of Tennessee A&I State College, Meharry Medical College, and Fisk University; H.A. Boyd's home on the border of Fisk's campus; the grave of his father in Greenwood Cemetery; and Harriet Albertine Boyd's home on Heiman Street "for lemonade."

In 1940, the Sunday School Congress met in San Antonio. In mid-April 1940, Boyd and Sadie B. Wilson made advance visits to San Antonio, where Boyd spoke at a citywide rally with the city's mayor. Earlier that day, Boyd and a five-car caravan had toured 22 Sunday Schools to urge them to attend the rally and support the National Baptist Sunday School which was set for June 5-9, 1940. The executive board of the National Baptist Convention of America also attended the Congress and made plans for their September 1940 convention in Louisville. They were expecting at least 500 preachers and pastors to attend the Congress.

In 1944, the Sunday School Congress met in Houston. The New England delegates had to leave home on Saturday, June 3, in order to make the railroad trip to the opening session on Wednesday, June

7. The Nashville group would need to leave on June 5 on the Pan American Flyer via New Orleans to Houston (*Nashville Globe*, June 2, 1944). Boyd presented a 72-page report on the NBPB and the Congress. The Sunday School Congress Band numbered 26 pieces, and the Congress Choir was comprised of 500 voices. Also in Houston, the NBCA's executive committee met and decided to hold the annual September NBCA session in Memphis at the Beale Street Baptist Church.

Although the war cut into attendance, the 1945 National Baptist Sunday School Congress met in Fort Worth with E.H. Branch, pastor of Olivet Baptist Church, serving as host pastor. Henry Allen Boyd directed the Congress to develop a "War Bond and Stamp Institute" to support America's war effort. Boyd said: "They, Christians, owe their country in doing all they can to hasten the end of the present war and also support the government agencies engaged in conservation measures." The various classes at the Congress were directed to discuss what the war meant to Christians and how to help conserve strategic products such as sugar, metal, and rubber. Boyd also discussed these subjects during the morning religious services at the Publishing Board. The NBPB eventually shipped religious materials across the world to military personnel, Lott Carey foreign mission workers, and churches in Panama.

In November 1944, Citizens Bank reached the goal of $1 million in capital and assets. (*Globe*, September 18, 1945). The bank was able to get customers to invest $50,000 in Christmas savings accounts, which were paid the second week in December. The Christmas club clerk said: "A nickel saved is a nickel made" (*Globe*, January 12, November 16, 1945). Boyd said the goals of the bank included, "strengthening the capital structure, increasing the service, and making this a community bank, even to the extent of banking by mail." Citizens Bank invested $715,450 in U.S. War Bonds and church mortgages, and Henry Allen Boyd and Citizens Bank often provided financial aid to churches and preachers.

George Albert Long, the pastor of Beale Street Baptist Church, served as host for the September 1944 NBCA session; however, the Baptist leaders learned Reverend Long was engaged in a heated confrontation with one of Tennessee's most influential political bosses, Edward H. Crump. "Boss Crump," as many called him, came to Memphis at age 15 from nearby Mississippi and became a successful businessman.

Crump entered politics and became mayor of the city from 1910-1916 with the help of campaign songs written by William C. Handy, "the father of the Blues." He reentered politics in 1917 as Shelby County's Treasurer and served two terms in the U.S. Congress from 1931-1935.

After becoming disgusted with congressional life, Crump returned to Memphis simply to be "Boss." No man could become mayor of Memphis, win local and county offices, or win the position of governor of Tennessee without the support of Crump and his political machine. This machine allegedly used collections from illegal prostitution, gambling, and the numbers racket to buy poll tax receipts ($2 each). The receipts were passed out to poor voters, including Negroes, who culled the Crump ticket in every election. Crump and his political machine reportedly used any means necessary, and this included strong use of local police to quiet his enemies and political opposition. Police accidentally killed several "uppity Negroes," including a federal employee (a Negro postman).

In 1939, Crump was elected into his final term as mayor. It was during this time that he and his machine forced Robert R. Church Jr. and his Lincoln League Republican Club into political submission. As a result, Church Jr. (d. 1952) fled to Chicago in November 1940. In 1941, the machine ordered the city fire department to burn the huge Church family mansion on Vance Avenue and allowed 2,000 people to watch the fire as a "demonstration of modern fire fighting equipment." The fire symbolically demonstrated what could happen if someone crossed Boss Crump. The city machine reportedly sent the police to harass two of Church's supporters, which forced them also to flee to Chicago.

Only George A. Long and a few other brave souls dared criticize the treatment of Church and his friends. In Boss Crump's town, the local chapter of the NAACP was defunct; and the organization effectively would not be revived until after Crump's death (1954).

The Reverend Long and the new head of the local National Urban League were determined to defy Jim Crow practices in the capital of the Mississippi Delta. New troubles began in Memphis in November 1943 when the machine had placed about 20 local Negro leaders in an empty downtown jail cell. Crump employed the police commissioner and the city attorney to lecture the local Negro leaders about potential race riots. He warned of negative consequences for all parties if the "radical Negro leader, A. Phillip Randolph" was allowed to come to Memphis and carry out a scheduled speech.

Randolph had been head of the Brotherhood of Sleeping Car Porters Union since the late 1920s; since the 1930s, he and the NAACP had led in pushing the New Deal federal administration to do more to protect and extend Negro civil rights. After meeting in the jail with city officials, these Negro leaders agreed to cancel the Randolph visit, according to the *Memphis World*, a weekly black newspaper.

At the request of black leaders, Randolph had to settle for a speech before the Southern Tenant Farmers Association at Greater White Stone Baptist Church on Wellington Street. He and the local Urban League president vowed to help more than a million impoverished Negro tenant farmers who toiled in the Delta. Many white and Negro tenants had been forced from the land between 1939 and 1944 because they formed a labor union for better wages and took their petition to Washington, D.C.

Thus, Randolph began mobilizing the labor unions in the South. This included stops in Nashville to tell Southern Negroes that registering to vote would place pressure on President Franklin D. Roosevelt (D) and both political parties to include civil rights initiatives in their 1944 election platforms. Randolph's threat to March on Washington with tens of thousands of protesters already had forced Roosevelt to issue the famous June 25, 1941, *Executive Order 8802*. This forbade employment discrimination in federal-related industries and created the President's Fair Employment Practices Commission. On August 28, 1963, Randolph finally helped carry out his "March on Washington" with Martin Luther King Jr.

In March 1944, the Reverend Long allowed Randolph to hold the mass meeting in Beale Street Baptist Church. When Randolph returned to Memphis and spoke, he said, "Boss Crump out— Hitler's Hitler." The police commissioner reportedly said he wished he had been there to "pull that Negro off that stage for talking about

Mr. Crump that way. Memphis is a white man's town, and anyone who disagrees had better move on."

Crump said George A. Long was desecrating the church by allowing outside agitators to disturb local race relations. Crump issued a veiled threat by saying Memphis would be better off without preachers like George Albert Long. The fiery Baptist preacher responded, "Now, as far as the town being better off without me, I did not ask Mr. Crump if I could come to this town, and I am not going to ask him if I may stay. Jesus Christ is my Boss."

In response, Crump's political machine had city codes "do an inspection of Beale Street Baptist Church," which cited thousands of dollars of needed corrective work on the old 1866 building. Boyd arranged for the NBPB and Citizens Bank to assist in paying for the work to meet city codes. Eventually, G.A. Long relocated to Detroit where he began leading Mt. Tabor Baptist Church. In a farewell note, the *Union-Review* (April 12, 1947) reported, "He has accomplished great good in Memphis."

Robert Church and George Long were just two of the millions of Negroes who fled the turbulent, oppressive, impoverished South. Long's coconspirator against Crump, the head of the Memphis Urban League, was removed by the national office and sent back to Chicago. The *Chicago Defender* said one could tell when there had been recent troubles or lynchings in the South because the buses and trains in Chicago would be filled with recent Negro arrivals. During the Great Migration, between 1890-1960, five million Negroes left the South. The greatest number of them left between 1940 and 1960. The daily *Chicago Defender* sent out calls for Negroes to abandon mistreatment in the South and come to the North. Places like Chicago, Detroit, Milwaukee, Cleveland, Toledo, East St. Louis, and other industrial towns soon had huge, thriving black communities complete with schools and many churches; therefore, the NBCA and the NBPB's Sunday School Congress began to schedule more of their annual sessions in Northern cities.

Crump died in August 1954, about three months after *Brown vs. Board of Education.* In this groundbreaking precedent, the U.S. Supreme Court decreed segregated schools were unconstitutional. When asked what E.H. Crump would have said about *Brown,* one of the Memphis newspapers reported Crump was a friend of the

Negro. A new day was coming, and the Publishing Board would profoundly be affected by the civil rights movements.

The 42nd NBPB Sunday School Congress was held in Chicago in 1946. Ebenezer Baptist Church hosted the event, and H. B. P. Johnson held the mass choir practices beginning in May. The mass meeting was held in DuSable High School, with E.H. Branch (Texas) delivering the sermon. H.A. Boyd, L.H. Simpson (Texas), and J.H. Turner (Nashville); and the youth led the parade from Vincennes Street to the high school. Again, Texas had the largest delegation of messengers.

There were 33 song books published by the NBPB, including *Celestial Showers* by William Roseborough (Texas). His book was the second song book published by the NBPB, followed by *Lasting Hymns* and the *National Baptist Anthem Series* by Carter, Tobias, and Isaac. The *National Baptist Hymnal* was selling for $8.00 a copy; and the *National Jubilee Melodies* (50 cents a copy) included Songs of a Burdened People, Songs of Redemption, and Songs of Oppression, such as "Swing Low Sweet Chariot," "Study War No More," "Steal Away to Jesus," and "Lord I Can't Turn Back Now."

William Pickens of the U.S. Treasury Department was the guest speaker and recognized Henry Allen Boyd for his leadership in directing War Bond drives in his community and among the Negro Baptists. Pickens also tried to allay the fears of citizens about the recent explosion of atomic weapons:

> A den of rattlesnakes live together ever so peaceably, solely because each snake is aware the other has a destructive weapon. The United States is just as afraid of being destroyed by atomic bombs as are the other nations (i.e., the Soviet Union).

While Mr. Pickens was in attendance, the delegates to the Sunday School Congress took this opportunity to sign petitions to ask the U.S. Senate not to seat Senator Theodore Bilbo of Mississippi, whom they considered to be a brutal racist (*Union-Review*, July 8, 1946).

The National Baptist Publishing Board installed new equipment in 1946. They began remodeling the plant by enlarging the rooms, adding fluorescent lighting, providing new equipment, and commissioning a life-size statue of R.H. Boyd facing east. Negro Baptists across the nation had contributed funds for the statue, and many showed up for its dedication. Nationally known Baptist preachers headed the R.H. Boyd Memorial Commission, which set the program and unveiling of the bronze statue for Sunday, March 16, 1946. Breakfast was in a dining car parked at Union Station; and it was followed by a reception in a Pullman parlor car, a sermon, a program at Mt. Olive Baptist Church, the laying of a wreath on Boyd's grave, and a dinner at Union Station.

The NBPB's Chorus performed a concert at the War Memorial Auditorium in Nashville in December 1946. For the 1947 Sunday School Congress in Detroit, the New Orleans delegates met with the Nashville delegation at the Louisville-Nashville Railroad station. The 1947 Congress theme was "One World, One Book." The Congress reserved six hotels in Detroit and used the Gotham Hotel as their headquarters. J.H.L. Smith, pastor of Chicago's Ebenezer Baptist Church, had the honor of giving the opening sermon; the Congress Chorus provided music for each night's service. The traditional 12 major subjects included "The Sunday School Congress: A Molder of Baptist History." J.B. Ridley, chairman of the NBPB, opened the session; G.L. Prince asked Detroit citizens to shun Communism because its ideology was at odds with American Christian principles. H.A. Boyd said, "Detroit obstructionists sought to belittle the Congress and keep the public from supporting it." Boyd was ecstatic with the turnout, and he gave the "I told you so" speech on Friday, the closing day. Fortunately, the 1948 Kansas City Congress was just as successful.

The 1949 Sunday School Congress was held in Dallas, June 8-12. The 12 topics included "Opportunities for Worship, Work, and Play in the Daily Vacation Bible School." The Reverend B.E. Joshua headed the Committee on Home Assignments, which was necessary in the segregated South. Messengers focused on raising money for the church in Panama, which R.H. Boyd had established long ago. The Panama church was damaged by tropical termites and had to be demolished. In memory of the NBPB's missionary there, R.H. Thorburne (a graduate of Benedict College), H.A. Boyd headed the fundraising effort.

The Congress was scheduled again for Chicago in 1950, and buses and special trains were used to transport the messengers from place to place. The theme was: "You cannot teach what you do not know; you cannot lead where you do not go." The twelve subjects focused on: "Thoughts and Sayings of the Congress." The next six Congress sessions met in San Francisco, Houston, Indianapolis, San Antonio, Kansas City, and Cleveland.

By the 1950s, the National Baptist Publishing Board was earning more than a half million dollars annually. This was a great amount of money at a time when many people made less than $30 a week and many employers were paying Negro domestics "$3 a day and carfare." The NBPB paid more than the hourly minimum wage of 75 cents to attract workers with better educational backgrounds.

Post-World War II inflation influenced the NBPB to affiliate with the Protestant Church Owned Publishers Association to gain reasonable prices for paper and supplies. Thus, the Publishing Board was able to continue publishing *Hope* magazine and the *Sunday School Lesson Commentary*. However, after the longtime editor, E.H. Borden, died, the NBPB was pressed to find a new editor for the *Commentary*. This book was a complex, expensive work that was designed to interpret and explain every quarter's lessons. The ministers and churches depended on this publication.

With slight economic depressions after World War II, the Publishing Board's problems with receiving bad checks grew worse. At the 1951 NBCA session, President Green L. Prince urged the delegates to do as Richard Henry Boyd had done: "Pool our own resources and build for ourselves," rather than beg other people to share their institutions.

In October 1952, Henry Allen Boyd became seriously ill and had to rely on his nephew, the assistant-secretary treasurer of the NBPB. T.B. Boyd, Jr. was the eldest son of Henry Allen's brother, T.B. Boyd, Sr. To better prepare his successor, Henry Allen approved the election of Boyd, Jr. in 1959 as one of the Publishing Board's directors. Henry A. Boyd had been including him in the board's meetings since 1951; and Boyd, Jr. had been elected to the Citizens Bank's board of directors in 1947. They had good relations with the NBCA, whose president said:

> During these years of progress [1935-1955], we have had the great hand of support at every turn of distress. We must feel as one family should feel towards another family that has given unselfish

support in helping to maintain and lead us to success, as has been the conduct of the NBPB and its secretary, Dr. Henry Allen Boyd, to the great Baptist family of the NBCA.

Henry Allen Boyd told local Negroes, via the *Globe*, to register and vote or "someone else will vote for you." He found that encouraging Negros to understand the importance of their rights was increasingly becoming important for the dissemination of the Civil Rights Movement.

T.B. Boyd, Jr. led the Congress parade into the arena in Kansas City, Missouri for the 49th session. The 1958 NBPB Sunday School Congress convened on June 11-15, in Fort Worth with its host, the Greater St. James Baptist Church; Henry Allen Boyd still was too ill to lead the procession. The Congress had evolved into departments of home and extension work, intermediate, juniors, Metoka and Galeda, music, cadet drills and exhibition, Sunday school superintendents, teacher training, and ushers. Other aspects of the Congress included workshops and independent exhibitors with church-related wares (including fine hats for the ladies, clothes, and accessories for church-going people). Also at Congress, the messengers were asked to meet a $7,000 goal to help rebuild the Panama church, where the widow, Bessie Thorburne, still served as the missionary.

The Great Migration northward was still strong and would not slow until 1960. Negro churches in the North were growing. F. Benjamin Davis had just laid the cornerstone for his New Bethel Missionary Baptist Church in Indianapolis; Moses McKissack of Nashville was the architect. Davis' church had hosted the Sunday School Congress in 1953, but the church was destroyed in a fire two years later. Davis was dean of the Central Baptist Theological Seminary in Indiana.

W.N. Daniel of Chicago led a march of 2,000 into the new edifice for the Antioch Missionary Baptist Church and held "Coming Home Services" on June 28, 1958. Daniel had succeeded J. Monroe James (1932-1957) at Antioch, according to the *Union-Review* (May 3, June 28, 1958).

The Southern black Baptist churches, especially those from Texas, were still strongest in drill team participation. The Boy Cadets organization was in its 48th year and had become the A.G. Cadet

Drill and Exhibition Teams. Many churches began to heavily invest in the competitions held at the annual Sunday School Congress sessions. The program was expensive, but the churches felt the investment was worth the money. It would guarantee exciting activities for its young members; bring more youngsters to the church; and provide them with discipline, group-related skills, and Christian morals.

On May 28, 1959, the death of Henry Allen Boyd signaled the end of an era and the beginning of a new one for the publishing company. At the 1959 Congress in Denver, Boyd, Jr. along with his wife and children, took charge of the session. Union Baptist Church served as host and welcomed messengers from 46 states. The Congress had last met there in 1931 when G.L. Prince was pastor. The 1959 Congress required 16 hotels, where they charged rates of $4 to $10 a day for a room with or without a bath.

Edna H. Porter of Los Angeles directed the "Pre-Congress Musical" where 250 voices with seven bands and musical groups performed on the first night; the "Henry Allen Boyd Brass Band" led the parade. The Congress included classes for band and orchestra. Messengers dedicated the Sunday School Congress session to the memory of Henry A. Boyd: "In the home-going of Dr. Henry Allen Boyd, in the light of his services to his day and generation, the race has lost a true symbol of Negro initiative" (*Union-Review* stated, June 6, 1959).

The overflowing funeral services for Dr. Henry Allen Boyd were moved from Mt. Olive Missionary Baptist Church to the auditorium of Tennessee A&I State University. Nashville's mayor and other dignitaries made remarks. The *Globe* continued publication until the first of January 1960. However, the Lincoln-Douglass Republican club Henry Allen had led soon died because Negro voters dramatically shifted to the Democratic Party in the November 1960 elections. Henry Allen Boyd was interred at Greenwood Cemetery. Around 1976, Tennessee State University named one of its newly built men's dormitories H.A. Boyd Hall after the fallen leader who was one of the original founders of the institution.

◄ Henry Allen Boyd, Secretary-Treasurer, NBPB, 1922-1959

▲ Wedding of Georgia Bradford and Henry Allen Boyd, 1908

◄ Henry Allen Boyd and Associates prepare for trip

National Baptist Publishing Board Plant, Nashville, 1920s ►

NBPB Headquarters, Nashville, 1950s ▼

Ebenezer Baptist Church ▶

Ebenezer
Groundbreaking ▶

◀ Ebenezer Baptist
Sunday School Band

◀ Golden Gems Book

Graduates E.H. Branch
and Dr. C. Clay ▶

▲ 1930 Convention, Chicago

▼ Henry Allen Boyd Band

◀ H.A. Boyd, T.B. Boyd, Jr., Sims & Eppse

Negro Doll Ad ▲

▲ Meharry Brass Band

National Escorts Congress:Dallas ▼

◀ Rev. G.L. Prince

Rev. J.B. Ridley ▶

◀ Rev. Henry Allen Boyd

◀ Ms. Sadie B. Wilson

Sunday School Literature ▼

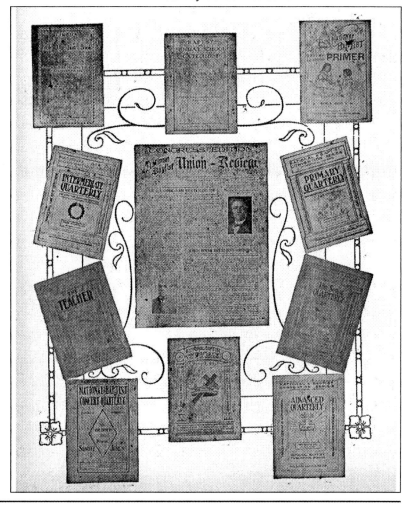

1. Rev. T.B. Boyd, Jr. at Rev. W.E. Hausey's church anniversary 1965.

2. Mrs. Georgia Boyd wife, of Dr. Henry A. Boyd in the 1950s.

3. Women stitching books at The National Baptist Publishing Board in the 1940s.

4. Presentation to Dr. Henry A. Boyd in the 1950s with T.B. Boyd Sr. on the right.

5. Men working at The National Baptist Publishing Board in the 1940s.

6. Gathering at Citizens Bank with Henry A. Boyd in the 1950s.

1

1. This brick mansion at 1602 Heiman St. in north Nashville was the home and place of death of African-American publishing, banking and religious leader Richard Henry Boyd.
2 "Boyd House" on the Fisk University campus, home of Henry Allen Boyd.
3. Richard Henry Boyd founder of the National Baptist Publishing Board and Citizens Bank.

1. Richard Henry Boyd with group in 1910.
2. Henry A. Boyd, right, president of Citizens Savings Bank and Trust Co., and his nephew and bank director T.B. Boyd Jr., standing next to him, welcome guests at a 50th anniversary open house in 1954. Others who were identified, from left, were Wilameana Bradford, J.R. Blake and M.G. Ferguson, the bank's executive vice president.
3. Henry Allen Boyd with group in 1925.

1959–1979
T.B. Boyd Jr.
and the New Era of the
Publishing Business

Except the Lord build the house, they labour in vain that build it; except the LORD keep the city, the watchman waketh but in vain.

— Psalms: 127:1, KJV

By the time T.B. Boyd, Jr. took control of the Publishing Board's operations, the Civil Rights Movement was shifting into a public forum. It was inevitable that the NBCA, the Publishing Board, and other black Baptist conventions and their members would become caught up in the Civil Rights Movement. After the 1955 Montgomery bus boycott, headed by a Baptist minister named Martin Luther King, Jr., the U.S. Supreme Court declared the city's segregated bus system unconstitutional in 1956. The president of the National Baptist Convention of America, the Reverend G.L. Prince, said to the September 1956 NBCA convention delegates:

The present condition through which we as a race are passing should encourage us as a group to take every advantage to assert our claim and right to full status of first-class citizens in this country for which our sons have bled and died. The day of the 'Uncle Tom' is gone forever.

On July 31, 1959, a group of youngsters from the National Baptist Convention of America attended summer workshops at the famed Highlander Folk School, which trained labor union leaders and civil rights leaders to create social change. One night, the Tennessee state police burst into the school, knocked out the lights, and made the workshop participants lie down on the floor; the troopers claimed they were looking for "illegal whiskey." One teenager was so afraid in the dark she began singing an old labor union song "We shall overcome," but she changed the words to "I am not afraid." The others took up the singing with her, "We are not afraid." Consequently, the song became an anthem for the Civil Rights Movement across the nation.

State officials in Tennessee, Georgia, and Arkansas became determined to shutdown Highlander. In Monteagle, Tennessee, Highlander decided to expand their union organizing and leadership training activities beyond helping poor white people in the mountainous regions into training leaders for the Civil Rights Movement. Tennessee revoked Highlander's state charter in 1960 and confiscated its properties. The state closed the school in 1961 for allegedly being a "subversive organization" selling whiskey and mixing the races at dances. Highlander officials unsuccessfully appealed to the U.S. Supreme Court; therefore, Highlander moved to Knoxville; got another charter under a modified name; purchased a facility in New Market, Tennessee; and continued operations.

At the September 1959 session of the NBCA, Boyd, Jr. said:

> It is with deep humility and with great appreciation that, I, your secretary, stand before you to make this report [on the NBPB] in place of my illustrious uncle, Dr. Henry Allen Boyd, who departed this life on May 28, 1959, and left a mark that neither time nor tide can ever erase. We lost one of the greatest leaders the world has ever produced.

M.C. Allen of Virginia Seminary was editor of the *Union-Review*, which included "Every Woman's Page." In the August 8, 1959 Union-Review, Boyd, Jr. published a large advertisement to assure customers the transition of leadership was smooth and the company would continue to give good service. The *Union-Review* stated:

> When Moses, the servant of God died, God knew it was necessary for another to take his place, as the work of a nation had to be carried on, so He chose another to take his place. Reverend T.B. Boyd, Jr., the nephew of the late Henry Allen Boyd has been elected by the Board as Secretary. We stand ready and willing to serve your every need.

Boyd, Jr. reported that the Publishing Board balanced its books at $758,642.37 with assets of $813,069.53. Declines in assets had occurred during the two recent recessions, but the company remained financially sound and productive. Boyd, Jr. began his career at the Publishing Board at an early age by working alongside his father in the composing room as a linotype worker; and this background helped him exponentially to grow the business into a successful, stable company.

Theophilus Bartholomew Boyd, Jr. (1917-1959) was born in Nashville, Tennessee, graduated from Pearl High School, attended Fisk University for a while, and finally graduated from Tennessee A&I State College in 1940. He served in the U.S. Army in the Pacific Theater of World War II. In 1941, he married Mable Louise Landrum who was the daughter of Jessie and Margaret (Jenkins) Landrum of nearby Wilson County. Mable Landrum attended Pearl High School and Tennessee A&I State College, majoring in home economics. Mable Boyd worked in local war industry factories while her husband was away in the war. They had four children: Theophilus B. III, Margaret Jerrilyn, Brenda Joyce, and William Allen. Their children attended and completed Tennessee State University.

Boyd, Jr. was ordained as a minister in 1956 and was the elected pastor of Greater Salem Baptist Church in Louisville, Kentucky. He diligently commuted more than 147,000 miles by air; and when he chose not to fly, Mable Boyd would drive the car for the three-hour trip while her husband did his work and wrote his notes. Boyd, Jr. was the first head of the NBPB to continue as a church pastor; and he served two different churches in that capacity.

As head of the NBPB, Boyd, Jr. continued to be involved in community and business affairs by becoming a member of Tau Lambda Chapter of the Alpha Phi Alpha Fraternity, the National Chamber of Commerce, the Metro Nashville Human Relations Commission, and president of Citizens Realty and Development Company. He was one of the first Negro members of the State Board of Regents which was chartered by the General Assembly in 1972 to help oversee public colleges and universities.

The 1960 "National Baptist Sunday School and B.Y.P.U. Congress," as it was then called, met in W.N. Daniel's Antioch Baptist Church in Chicago. The Pre-Congress Musical took place on June 13 in Soldiers' Field Stadium. The NBCA and NBPB officers took a photograph with Dr. Martin Luther King, Jr. who was one of the speakers.

Dr. King and his Southern Christian Leadership Conference required the loyalty of many Negro churches. Therefore, the Reverend Kelly Miller Smith and other ministers organized the Nashville Christian Leadership Council (NCLC) to be affiliated with the SCLC in 1958. This was essential in mobilizing local churches of all denominations in support of the Civil Rights Movement. The NCLC supported the Nashville Student Movement (1959-1964), which launched downtown sit-in demonstrations from the basement of First Colored Baptist. The college students and others from across the South met at Raleigh in April 1960 and formed the Student Nonviolent Coordinating Committee (SNCC) with the help of King's SCLC. The strategist for the Nashville movement was a Methodist preacher by the name of Reverend James Marion Lawson, Jr. He developed the objectives and philosophy for SNCC, and many of the community mass meetings were held in local churches of all denominations.

The National Baptist Convention U.S.A., Incorporated (NBCI) neither supported civil disobedience tactics nor Dr. King's leadership in the Civil Rights Movement. The head of the NBCI considered such tactics as non-Christian. However, the president of the NBPB-affiliated NBCA said in 1961, "I desire the rights, the privileges that the Constitution of the United States grants me." The NBCI ended its September 1961 session with a tumultuous fight over the undemocratic process of electing the convention's president. King was ousted as a NBCI officer, and the turmoil led to the formation of the Progressive National Baptist Convention, Inc., which was formed in Cincinnati's Zion Baptist Church on November 15, 1961 and incorporated on May 10, 1962.

T.B. Boyd, Jr. was deeply concerned about the Negro Baptist divisions. He believed the disputes were because of the "lack of focus on religion—the real business at hand." He decried the religious and lay Negro leaders on their inability, morally and economically, to help uplift the black people of America. Boyd knew religious splits perpetuated deep personal resentment and group hatred. He also knew that emotional baggage would linger for decades and prevent sensible reunification of America's black Baptists.

In the early 1960s, the Sunday School Congress met in Portland, Oregon; Houston; Kansas City, Missouri; and Chicago.

Boyd convened the Second Annual Congress Conductors meeting in Nashville in December 1964 in the NBPB's department of Christian education to discuss the National Baptist Sunday School Congress. C.D. Pettaway was present. Boyd wanted to "iron out differences and wrinkles" in order to help Congress more smoothly operate:

> Such meetings will result in clarifying the purpose and program of the Congress, and will enable us to launch a greater unified effort through our newly adopted program of Christian Education in the Sunday School and Baptist Training Union Congress, as we seek to reach and supply the needs of many unreached and unenlisted men, women, and children throughout our nation.

Samuel H. Simpson was a native of Texas and a graduate of Guadalupe College. He became pastor of Lake Providence Missionary Baptist Church on November 6, 1931. He was also chairman of the NBPB, secretary of the Nashville Colored YMCA, and general secretary of the Stones River Missionary Baptist District Association for 40 years. Under Simpson, the church became a bevy of activity. He retired the mortgage on the building and brought dozens of new members into the congregation. In the farthest southern end of Nashville-Davidson County, Simpson led the Lake Providence congregation from its old building to a new one in September 1951; he continued to serve as pastor until he died on February 18, 1976.

The 1965 Sunday School Congress was scheduled to meet in Oakland, California. The session was hosted by the Evergreen Baptist Church during June 16-20. From 1966 to 1969, the Sunday School Congress met in New Orleans' Freeman's Baptist Church (1966), Cincinnati's First Shiloh Baptist Church (1967), Houston's First Shiloh Baptist Church (1968), and Chicago's Antioch Baptist Church (1969).

Tragedies and triumphs continued to plague the turbulent 1960s. President J.F. Kennedy (D) was murdered in November 1963, soon after the March on Washington. "The Church and Social Action" are necessary in the midst of the Civil Rights Revolution," the *Union-Review* stated (December 5, 1964). The militant leader Malcolm X was assassinated in a Northern ghetto in 1965. When the bellicose SNCC president Stokely Carmichael came to speak in Nashville in April 1967, youngsters and police engaged in two days of rioting. Throughout these times, the U.S. Congress and President Lyndon B. Johnson (D) approved the Civil Rights Act of 1964, the Voting Rights Act of 1965, and the Open Housing Act of 1968.

When Dr. King was assassinated in Memphis on April 4, 1968, the *Union-Review* carried memorable pictures of him and parts of his most recognized speeches. After being contacted by the National Council of Churches of Christ, T.B. Boyd, Jr. sent a letter asking black pastors to help prevent more rioting from occurring in reaction to King's assassination. Boyd said, "There are good things that have happened as a result however; and that is, the unmasking of white America and the fact that white Americans have been forced to take a good look at themselves, as well as the prevalent social system which has created the climate for these [urban] disturbances."

Unfortunately, situations for the U.S. worsened. The Vietnam War that was raging in Southeast Asia became so controversial at home that it caused discord in the streets of American cities and contributed to President Johnson's refusal to run for reelection. The subsequent split in the liberal Democratic Party allowed the conservative Republicans to elect a two-term president, Richard M. Nixon (R).

After the Civil Rights Acts were passed, many white companies sought business from black churches; however, few white customers bought products and services from black businesses. In the Era of Integration, blacks were no longer a loyal clientele of black businesses and became patrons of the better financed, more convenient, and more price efficient white businesses and publishers. The NBPB was forced to change and modernize in order to successfully compete.

Fortunately, T.B. Boyd, Jr. already had begun to change company procedures and products. He improved the quality of publications and allowed no more commercial advertisements in the products. He bought new printing machines and planned for a two-color press. The NBPB had an increase in revenues and assets in 1960 after three years of decline. In 1961, the company's assets reached $950,006. In 1962, the company was able to install new machinery; and the old National Baptist Church Supply Company facility was remodeled with composing rooms, a bindery, and proofreading rooms to expand the Publishing Board operations. In 1963, the company's assets reached $1.1 million and grew to $1,667,680 by 1969.

The old Publishing Board plant on 2nd Avenue consisted of several old houses, outbuildings, and additions; but it was no longer adequate. The city also had begun urban renewal projects and building interstate highways in the two decades since World War II. The old plant downtown was in the middle of an urban renewal area where almost all the black businesses and homes were destroyed between 1947 and 1970. Out of seven historic black churches dating back to 1833, only First Colored Baptist Church remained downtown by 1972. The Boyd family church, Mt. Olive, moved to Albion Street across from Tennessee State University in the early 1960s. T.B. Boyd, Jr. employed his eldest son, T.B. Boyd III who was a graduate of Tennessee State, to begin plans for building a new million dollar plant on 4.5 acres in an industrial park on Centennial Boulevard in West Nashville. This new plant was two miles west of the Tennessee State campus.

In December 1974, the National Baptist Publishing Board moved into the new facility at 6717 Centennial Boulevard. The production facilities were well-lit and spacious, and it had safety zones to protect the workers. The machines were modern and supported by the latest technology, and the portion of the complex dedicated to management and editorial offices was spacious. The new design included a large conference room, a modern chapel, a two-story reception area with a welcome and information desk, a small bookstore, and offices for administrators. The parking, unlike downtown at the old buildings, was paved with plenty of room for cars, loading docks for trucks, and visitors' buses and cars.

On April 1, 1979, T.B. Boyd, Jr. passed away in the hospital after suffering an illness. He left behind his wife and four children (Jerrilyn Boyd Hadley, Brenda Boyd Wooding, T.B. Boyd III, and William Allen Boyd); his father, T.B. Boyd, Sr.; a sister, Rose Evelyn Morgan; and brothers, James Calvin Boyd of St. Louis and Elwood Boyd of Washington, D.C.; and grandchildren: T.B. Boyd IV, Rodney and Michelle Hadley, and Ronald Wooding. Patton Brothers Funeral Home conducted the funeral at Mt. Olive Baptist Church on Albion Street on Tuesday at 4:00 p.m.; and Marcel Kellar, pastor at Mt.

Olive, presided. W.N. Daniel traveled from Chicago to give the eulogy. The burial took place at Nashville's Woodlawn Cemetery (*The Tennessean*, April 3, 1979). At the September 5, 1979, NBCA session, the president of the National Baptist Nurses Corps Auxiliary referred to him as, "a very dear friend and brother, . . . a great national figure, and a nobleman." She also added, "Wednesday, April 1, 1979, is an epoch-marking day in National Baptist history."

At this point, the National Baptist Publishing Board was 83 years old; and its future never had been brighter. Although the balance sheet fell during the nation's severe economic recession of 1974, the NBPB bounced back with a balance of $1.03 million in 1975. Through those 83 years of history, the company had only three presidents; and each one of them earned great respect throughout the nation. Even those African Americans who did not do business with the Publishing Board were proud the company reflected well upon all the people. Many were thankful that at least one black business and Christian agency among them was stable, financially able, and competitive in the American economy.

The Publishing Board continued taking the Sunday School Congress to various cities: Kansas City, Missouri's St. Stephen Baptist Church (1970); Jackson, Mississippi's Friendship Baptist Church under the Reverend L. Blankenship (1971); Detroit's Galilee Baptist Church and Convention Center (1972); Indianapolis' New Bethel Baptist Church and the Indiana Convention Exposition Center (1973); and Ft. Worth's Mt. Olive Baptist Church (1974).

The use of hotels and large convention centers had become common for messengers and officers of the Publishing Board. The 1975 National Baptist Sunday School and Baptist Training Union Congress convened in Wichita on June 11-16. This Congress, which was sponsored by the Macedonia Missionary Baptist Church, attracted 11,000 participants and visitors. The revenue from messengers and guests was an economic boom for the host cities. As a result, many cities and their tourism bureaus began to see the NBPB's Sunday School Congress as a necessary asset for local economic growth.

▲ Dr. T.B. Boyd, Jr., Secretary-
Treasurer, NBPB (NBR)

T.B. Boyd, Jr. ▲.

Mrs. T.B. Boyd, Jr.
(Mable Landrum) ▼

◀ NBPB Publication for Children
(T.B. Boyd, Jr.'s children)

NBPB Employees
Working in Old Plant ▶

◀ NBPB Employees in the Old
Plant (T.B. Boyd, Sr. at far
left, back row)

▲ T.B. Boyd, Jr. Visits Church
Ewing and Oscar Crawford at
New Printing Machines

◀ Gilbert King Adjusts a Printing
Press at Old NBPB

▲ T.B. Boyd, Jr., Church Leaders Talk

▲ Employees Adjust Machines at Publishing House, Nashville

◀ Dr. Richard H. Dixon, Sr. with
President Lyndon Johnson

▼ Rev. J. Royster Powell

▼ T.B. Boyd Jr. and Dr. Dixon with Statue

▲ Dr. M.L. King, Jr. with T.B. Boyd, Jr. in Chicago

N.Y. Pro. Bap. Con. Leaders ▲

1. R.H. Boyd with Mt. Olive Missionary Baptist Church congregation in the 1890s.

2 Pressman, Gilbert King in the early 1960s.

3. Chuck Ewing, Oscar Crawford and Rev. T.B. Boyd Jr. standing by the press in the early 1960s.

4. Bindery department in the 1930s - 1940s.

1. National Baptist Publishing Board on Second Avenue.

2 Typesetting Department in the 1950s–1960s.

3. H.A. Boyd with group of women in the 1920s.

4. Statue of R.H. Boyd.

5. Second Class Mailing Department in the 1930s.

CHAPTER SEVEN

1979–1996
T.B. Boyd III Takes the NBPB to the End of the First 100 Years

Although the mantle has fallen on my shoulders, I will not let it hit the ground. —Theophilus Bartholomew Boyd III

In April 1979, the board of directors elected Theophilus B. Boyd III as the new head of the National Baptist Publishing Board. He had worked at the NBPB since 1963 as a high school student and joined the company after graduating from Tennessee State University in 1969. He had been around the NBPB's plant since the age of four, and he among few other youngsters in the family had taken his father's work with all seriousness. His great-uncle, Henry Allen, had died 10 years prior, and his great-grandfather, Richard Henry Boyd, had died decades earlier. Young Boyd III was observant and studious, gathering all the stories and history of his family, listening to the conversations, and looking at the actions of the NBPB's leaders. He attended with his family the annual Sunday School Congress sessions, helped to operate them, and got to know the great Baptist preachers in that noble clan, the National Baptist Convention of America. He was groomed and nurtured for leadership by his father, who had carefully consulted the trusted preachers on the NBPB's board of directors and the pastors at the annual meetings of the Sunday School Congress and the NBCA. T.B. Boyd, Jr. knew he needed the most influential leaders in the NBCA to support any successor at the National Baptist Publishing Board.

In 1974, T.B. Boyd III became personnel director at the Publishing Board. On November 3, 1976, he was elected to the NBPB's board of directors. In 1978, he became assistant secretary of the NBPB. The first great test for T.B. Boyd III was the design and completion of the

$1 million new plant. He did this with ease, and even designed new NBPB products. In the year T.B. Boyd Jr. died, the Publishing Board balanced the books with $2,420,885.44.

Fate and history—these elements seemed to be the guardian angels for the Publishing Board and the Boyd family. Like his father had done in June 1959, young T.B. Boyd III eagerly addressed the Sunday School Congress almost exactly 20 years later. He said,

> It is a day of peace, a day of tranquility, a day of progress, and a day of recommitment to the very principles our forefathers laid down before us. Although the mantle has fallen on my shoulders, I will not let it hit the ground.

He took a deep breath. The older leaders seemed to accept this 32-year-old youngster as the new leader of the Sunday School Congress and the Publishing Board.

After returning from the convention and catching his breath, T.B. Boyd III sat at the desk in his sunlit office. He was reflecting on the awesome position in which he found himself, and how the National Baptist Publishing Board had survived for nearly 85 years. He thought about his grandfather, Richard Henry Boyd, who had to hire a white man to buy a printing press for him because nobody in Nashville would sell such machinery to a Negro. Boyd III thought about his father's years of toil, and he thought about his great-uncle, Henry Allen Boyd, who for more than fifty years dazzled the crowds with his white suits and white shoes in dozens of annual Congress parades. In 1979, there were even more black Baptist conventions and keener competition from black and white companies in an entirely new business and market economy than when his predecessors managed the Publishing Board. The National Baptist Publishing Board still was the largest black publishing company of religious material in the city. Boyd III was the fourth generation leader, and the mantle indeed rested on his shoulders.

Newspaper reporters interviewed him and came to see if the NBPB was surviving. The 32-year-old Boyd III reminded a *Nashville Banner* reporter he was placed in an elected position and not in an inherited one. "I had to be a fighter to a certain degree to get where

I am now. Now that I'm here, I am going to have to fight harder to keep the business going and growing like I want it to." He recalled the old downtown site of the NBPB was near the former auction blocks and brokerage houses where slaves were housed for sale and loaned money at 6 percent per annum in antebellum times. Now, he, the great-grandson of former slaves, was operating a multimillion dollar company, built by his ancestors, to serve black Baptists across the world. Boyd III diverted the reporter's attention to the modern publishing plant, taking him on a tour to see the newest computers, the fastest printers, and the neat and professional employees, according to the *Nashville Banner* (November 21, 1979). Boyd meant to keep the Publishing Board at the edge of competition in religious publishing in order to market materials and services across the globe to whites and blacks, to Baptists and other Christians, and to churches and non-secular customers. Indeed, he meant to see the company through its 100th birthday!

The Publishing Board and the Sunday School Congress would reach dizzying heights in the next quarter-decade. As a business major in college, T.B. Boyd III had learned to apply sound business practices, business strategies, and long-range planning. One of his first successes was the development of the new *National Baptist Hymnal* (1977), which sold millions of copies by the 1980s. His attractiveness and charisma would help build valuable business and religious networks and cultivate good civic, denominational, and community relations to help advance the National Baptist Publishing Board.

Again, soon after the board elected him head of the company in April, the Sunday School Congress met in Chicago on June 12-17, 1979. W.N. Daniel and his Antioch Missionary Baptist Church on Englewood Street hosted the Congress, including the theme "Biblical Teachings for Contemporary Men" (Matthew 28:19-20). Daniel was a personal friend to T.B. Boyd, Jr. and had promised the dying father he would look after the young executive. Daniel became pastor of Antioch Missionary Baptist Church in 1967. By 1973, he was president of the Chicago chapter of the NAACP.

W.N. Daniel was a civil rights pioneer in his own right. He was the first Negro to attend Austin Peay State University in Clarksville, Tennessee. He had moved to Nashville to pastor the Pilgrim

Emmanuel Baptist Church, enrolled at American Baptist Theological Seminary, and then finished Tennessee A&I State University. After the announcement of *Brown vs. Board of Education* (1954), Daniel, who was born in nearby Kentucky, went to the president of Austin Peay and said he wanted to enroll in school. He received a master's degree from Austin Peay in 1956. Only the University of Tennessee in Knoxville had been forced by a suit filed by the NAACP (*Gray vs. UT*, 1951) to admit Negro graduate students. Vanderbilt University in Nashville had admitted a few Negroes into its graduate divinity program, and Negroes were suing Memphis State University in order to obtain undergraduate admission by the mid-1950s. Daniel, therefore, really was a brave pioneer in the desegregation of higher education in Tennessee.

With Daniel, and later F. Benjamin Davis, at his side, young Boyd III continued his father's rule not to allow people to use the Congress to pass hats and raise money for sundry causes and programs, although this rule caused grumbling among some individuals. The Chicago session involved 16,000 messengers and guests. In his presidential address, Boyd encouraged the audience to "live a life of commitment to God, to stand tall, reaching, teaching, and keeping." Reflecting the new leadership, the Publishing Board, the National Missionary Baptist Convention of America, and the Sunday School Congress supported a resolution to oppose the lifting of sanctions against the racist government of South Africa and supported the SCLC's call to raise the issue of high unemployment of black youth. Joyce Brown of the intermediate class of the Macedonia Baptist Church of Richmond, California, said, "As black people we have a deep understanding of what slavery meant to the Israelites." She urged her fellow youth to "believe in Him. Salvation will be yours—only Jesus alone," according to the *Union-Review* (April 7, 1979).

Under Theophilus B. Boyd III, the Sunday School Congress expanded rapidly and soon had to be reorganized and modernized. Preparations for the annual event and the on-site Congress operations demanded a staff member's full attention. The time required to book hotels, schedule transportation, secure the best available rates, negotiate with the convention hall staff for each event's setup, operate within the host city's rules and regulations, and communi-

cate with the host pastor and his church to provide certain amenities for the Congress participants took a year's time. The successful
Congress would depend on the effective work of the host
committee, which dealt with making arrangements for transportation, publicity, music, souvenir books, hospitality, finances, and
church services. The latter committee was in charge of planning and
directing the popular evening and late night services, which usually were held in the hotel ballroom or a room in the convention hall.
The most famous preachers were engaged for these services, usually addressing a packed house for three nights. After the last meeting
ended on Friday night, only months remained to finalize plans for
next year's Congress.

A more formal Congress Commission was formed to decide the
annual program and format. This structure, which was one of the
late T.B. Boyd, Jr.'s legacies, allowed more input from the denominational convention. The Youth Convention became a large part of
the week's activities, especially the spiritual dance contests, drill
competitions, oratory contests, classes, and scholarship presentations. In the early 80s, the Congress was hosted by Dallas' People's
Missionary Baptist Church, Cleveland's Sardis Missionary Baptist
Church, St. Louis' New Tower Missionary Baptist Church, and
Orlando's Mt. Pleasant Missionary Baptist Church.

Boyd III did not become involved so visibly in local political
leadership as Republicans Henry Allen and R.H. Boyd had done.
Like his father, Boyd Jr., Boyd III remained out of politics. After all,
the African Americans were no longer predominantly Republicans
as they had been from 1867 to 1959. Boyd III, like many young
African Americans, was impressed by a black presidential candi-
date, Jesse Jackson, a colleague of the late Dr. King. Boyd III said,
"We had a black man who stood and defied the thinking of America
as a whole and emerged with much the same pride for his people as
David did with Goliath." Boyd became a member of Kappa Alpha
Psi Fraternity, chairman of the board of directors of Citizens Bank
and Trust Company, and a trustee and vice chairman of the Board of
Trustees at Meharry Medical College for more than twenty years,
making him the senior member. He became Sir Archon (president)
of the Chi Boule Chapter of Sigma Pi Fraternity — the oldest (1904-
present) and most prestigious of African-American fraternities.

While president of the latter fraternity, he quickly brought new blood into the organization, which celebrated its 100th birthday in June 2004—the same year Citizens Bank would turn 100 years old. He was listed in several *Who's Who* publications, chaired the United Negro College Fund telethon in Middle Tennessee, and served as either head of or a member of a host of other programs. He was listed in several local and national publications as one of the most influential men in his community. His burden was just as great as that which had been placed on his predecessors at the Publishing Board.

By 1981, the National Baptist Publishing Board balanced its books with a record $3,453,980 during those perilous economic times. The Republican presidents had reigned since 1968, black poverty had risen to 34 percent despite the Democrats' recent "War on Poverty," and there were significant economic recessions during the next decade. Yet, Boyd III noticed the political climate had improved since the Civil Rights Movement because a number of blacks, including one from Tennessee (a fellow Tennessee State graduate, Harold E. Ford), served in the U.S. Congress (1974-1996). In what seemed to be the nadir of the Civil Rights Movement in the 1980s, blacks were pushing for more political power and the promotion of more educational opportunities in order to fully realize the remaining goals of the movement.

There was a great push to get more blacks into colleges and universities. According to the *Detroit Free Press* (May 8, 1983), between 1970 and 1980, the number of blacks in such institutions increased from 350,000 to 660,000. Due to the Civil Rights Movement's opening new educational opportunities in white institutions, America's Historically Black Colleges and Universities (HBCUs) held only 16 percent of black college students. The HBCUs produced a quarter of all black college graduates and 80 percent of black doctors. Boyd III and his mother, Mable Louise Boyd, therefore, met the crisis by establishing the T.B. Boyd, Jr. Scholarship and a $300,000 Endowment Fund. Boyd III said, "Because we care, we get involved and put back into the community in a creative, positive, and helpful way." Mable Boyd joined the board of directors for the NBPB, becoming chairperson of the T.B. Boyd, Jr. scholarship and endowment fund operations.

She served on the board of the Grace Eaton Home and worked closely with her daughter, Brenda, and son, William Allen, to help Boyd III with the annual Sunday School Congress operations.

To commemorate African-American History Month, the *Union-Review* published a February 3, 1983, sermon, "The Triumph of God in Black History," by the late Kelly Miller Smith (d. 1984), pastor of First Baptist Church, Capitol Hill. Smith said,

> Surely God triumphs in our history through our achievements...Look at the great heroes of faith who were God's sunburned children. God has triumphed in our history through the church...When we find ourselves oppressed by those who hate us, when we find ourselves trampled down by those who sit in the seats of power, the Bible speaks to us through the psalmist: 'The Lord is my light and salvation, whom shall I fear? The Lord is the strength of my life; of whom shall I be afraid?' I want you to know how it is that He understands all of the problems which beset us...God has triumphed in our history, and He will triumph in our lives, if we are willing to allow Him to take over the reins of our lives.

Black History Month always was dutifully observed at the NBPB, and Boyd III often was a speaker for many religious and lay organizations during that month. Retaining one of R.H. Boyd's traditions, the board's staff was always conscious of history, perhaps because "historical amnesia," as Frederick Douglass termed the malady, was costly to black people.

In 1984, Boyd III married Yvette Duke. After being engrossed in building a career in teaching, Yvette settled down to being a supportive wife. They had three children: LaDonna Yvette, Shalae' Shantel, and Justin Marriel. Boyd's oldest son, T.B. Boyd IV, from the first marriage, completed Florida A&M State University and attended school in New Jersey to complete his M.B.A. Yvette joined many boards, including Girl Scouts, Hermitage, and membership in Alpha Kappa Alpha Sorority, Links (The Links, Inc.), and Faith Unlimited. She attended Tennessee State University, earning bachelor's and master's degrees, teaching some courses, and completing substantial course work toward her doctorate. She was quoted in

"Celebrating 10 Years of Family and Community," Nashville, *Tennessee Tribune* (June 1994):

> I see to it that Dr. Boyd has a life away from the office and a pleasant home filled with love, so that when he goes to the office, he can do his best...T.B. is the head, and I am the heart [of the family].

Kind, warm, and personable, Yvette Boyd became a recognized civic and social leader, serving as a member of the Board of Overseers for the Vanderbilt University Ingram Cancer Center, according to *Momentum* (Summer 2003).

Dr. Boyd III was offering his expertise and services locally, across the state, and nationally. Many National Baptists looked to him for words of wisdom as a speaker in their churches, workshops, local and state conventions, and through his columns in the *National Baptist Union-Review*. His travel schedule was heavy, but he often was accompanied by his wife and sometimes by the children, when their school schedules permitted them to be away.

The National Baptist Sunday School and Baptist Training Union Congress was held in Denver, with the Radisson Hotel at 1550 Court Place as the headquarters, on June 11-16, 1985. The theme was "Christian Education: The Awareness of Many Gifts and the Knowledge of One God" (based on Ephesians 4:4-8). Dr. A.L. Bowman, pastor of Union Baptist Church, served as host, with El Ray Johnson serving as co-host. R.H. Gholson chaired the Tuesday night musical, and H.A. Alexander directed transportation. Bowman was vice president of the local chapter of Operation PUSH. Boyd III said:

> I stand before this great [1985] Congress and tell you the young people are the future. These little children . . . are the ones who are going to have to finish much of what we start. We must invest in our young people and make them a part of what we are about. Our young people of today will be the world of tomorrow.

Boyd III and his staff formalized the name change to National Baptist Sunday Church School and Baptist Training Union Congress after adding divisions for children, youth, and young adults (ages 4-24). The youth section became the Mini-Congress. The Congress continued to focus on Christian education training through the National Baptist Publishing Board and its publications, materials, and services. The NBPB had opened a second bookstore in Dallas. Dr. S.M. Lockridge was vice president of the National Baptist Convention of America. The T.B. Boyd, Jr. Essay Contest awarded $1,500 scholarships at the annual Sunday School Congress.

On June 11, 1986, at the Convention Center in New Orleans, hundreds of the expected 20,000 messengers already were seated, the music was playing, the drill teams in their colorful uniforms were moving down the aisles to their places, and thousands entered the doors to further charge the atmosphere—"It is Congress time!" St. John Institutional Church was the host. The mayor of New Orleans gave the welcoming remarks. Before Boyd spoke, his wife, Yvette Duke, 14-month-old daughter, LaDonna, and the baby, Shalaé, along with Dr. Boyd's special guests, several of whom traveled from Nashville to support him, were introduced on the stage. Boyd was introduced with a standing ovation. Dressed in his immaculate white suit and shoes, like his late Uncle Henry Allen Boyd, Boyd III reminded the audience, "We cannot forget the past." He asked the audience to "keep [their] egos low and spirits high and practice the Christian message." Walter Fauntroy, congressional representative from D.C., was the keynote speaker. B.F. Davis presided, Ruth L. Davis served as National Congress Chorister, and W.E. Hausey, pastor of St. John Institutional Missionary Baptist Church, was the host.

Boyd III's friend, David Satcher, president of Meharry Medical College, where Dr. Boyd served on the board of trustees, had some encouraging words published in the National Baptist Union-Review (February 1986), titled "Thinking of Ourselves." Satcher talked of his experiences as a Sunday school teacher at First Baptist Church, Capitol Hill of Nashville. Satcher taught his Sunday school students that a Christian should acquire a positive self-attitude as well as high regard for and high expectations of themselves and others. "As Christians, we are directed and admonished to think and act positively," said Satcher, who became U.S. Surgeon General.

The United States suffered a tremendous loss when the space shuttle exploded on launch and killed the entire crew. T.B. Boyd III offered sympathy, prayers, and pensive reflection to his constituents regarding the disaster: "The scene of the explosion . . . will remain with us for many years to come. This scene is a reminder that technology is still in God's hands, and though life was lost and hearts broken, the fact remains God knows best." He urged prayers for the families and the souls of the astronauts through the *Union-Review* (February 1986).

At the 81st Annual National Baptist Sunday Church School and Baptist Training Union Congress, held on June 16-21, 1987, in Dallas at the city convention center, a huge Congress Choir gave a soul-stirring concert at the Tuesday night musical. The drill team exhibitions were absolutely fascinating to visitors who had never seen this tradition of the African-American church. Dozens of drill teams performed, with some units from Texas having enough members to constitute a real military company. The children's drill team uniforms dazzled in the lights, and their recitation of Bible verses drew applause from the adult audience. There were massive crowds on each day at the session, and the exhibition hall was filled with rows of vendors and food stands. Some colleges and universities had student recruitment booths in the exhibition hall. There were huge buses from across the country, emblazoned with the name of the church or company. Children ran back and forth, laughing and shouting their approval of "Congress time!" According to tradition, the adults were dressed in their finest and newest outfits on the night of the musical. It surely was a fashion show to see. The Publishing Board's Department of Christian Education introduced the Certificate Program to accommodate congresses at the national, state, district, and local levels. Dr. S.M. Wright, president of the Missionary General Baptist Conference of Texas, was the host for the 81st Sunday School Congress.

In 1988, the NBCA president began to formulate a printing association with another company and organized youth and adult congresses. Many members protested this move and organized the National Missionary Baptist Convention of America, or "NMBCA," which reflected the doctrines and values of the old Baptist religion. The National Baptist Publishing Board left the National Baptist Convention of America and continued the printing and publishing arrangements with the National Missionary

Baptist Convention of America and the sponsoring of the historic Sunday School Congress.

At the 82nd Congress, Boyd III said,

We have, by faith and by worship, come to the point of seeing to it the truth in our Congress theme becomes meaningful action, not just mere words. If our theme, 'The Family: God's Prescription for Reflecting on the Past, Instructions for the Present, and Fulfillment of the Future' (based on Deuteronomy 6:6-7, 20, 25), is to serve the Congress, it must permeate the mind, soul, and being of the messengers to such a searing degree that it will spread to the thousands and thousands who come to them in Sunday Church schools and Baptist Training Unions to learn higher and higher ways to serve the Lord. That is the ultimate goal of the Congress. May God bless us all, and welcome to Nashville, from your servant in Christ, the National Baptist Publishing Board.

The mayor of Nashville-Davidson County welcomed the crowd, saying, "The history of the National Baptist Congress and this community have been intertwined throughout recent decades. National leaders have emerged from these communities who have contributed greatly to the success of the Congress."

The 1989 Sunday School Congress was held in Columbus, Ohio, and hosted by G. Thomas Turner and the Friendship Missionary Baptist Church. This session was held in the city convention center, which overflowed with messengers, participants, and visitors. The Congress theme was "The Family: God's Plan for Mankind," based on Jeremiah 31:1. Mable L. Boyd led the panel of judges for the T.B. Boyd, Jr. Scholarship Contest. The opening Sunday morning session was held at Friendship Missionary Baptist Church on West Broad Street. F. Benjamin Davis, chairman of the NBPB and Dean of the National Congress School of Methods, presided. The National Baptist Sunday Church School and B.T.U. Congress was considered a "School of Methods in which thousands of messengers gather annually to receive intensive training in Christian education." Southern Baptist Extension Seminaries accepted the adult courses. The NBPB reception took place on Monday evening, and the musical followed on Tuesday evening. The official Congress session began on Wednesday at 8:30 a.m. in the convention hall.

Within a complex and modern religious reformation, the formation of the National Missionary Baptist Convention of America (NMBCA) and its affiliation with the National Baptist Publishing Board in 1988 really were attempts at "restoration" and trying to hold on to the more traditional black Baptist faith. On September 4, 1989, the leaders of the NMBCA, the NBPB, and 400 others attended a "Unity Banquet" at the Reverend Daniels' church. T.B. Boyd III spoke and reminded the delegates, "God still is in the blessing business."

The first session of the NMBCA opened on September 6, 1989, in Chicago's Palmer House Hotel. Ruth Saul and Articia Matthews played the welcoming music as the delegates filled the meeting hall. More than 8,000 people crowded the McCormick Center in Chicago for the musical. Thousands sat shoulder-to-shoulder in the Grand Ballroom of the Palmer House. W.N. Daniel and his church hosted the session. Benjamin L. Hooks, executive director of the NAACP, was the featured speaker. Boyd III said, "When we combine the efforts of the Congress and the Publishing Board, along with the work of the Convention, we are unmatched. God is still in the blessing business." There was great applause! The Winter Board and Foreign Mission Board meetings were held Phoenix in February 1991. The first president of the NMBCA, Dr. S.M. Lockridge, said, "We are a Christian community working fearlessly in the Lord's vineyard. We have no fear, only faith that says if the Lord is with us, nothing and no one can defeat us."

On December 9-12, 1991, black church leaders met in Detroit for the Annual Consultation of the Congress of National Black Churches, Inc. (CNBC). There was concern that as the black church became more splintered, so did the African-American family and its communities. Seventy-two percent of black families were composed of a husband and wife in 1960, but only 38 percent of black families would have two heads of household by the end of the 1990s. With one head of household, the black family's average income dropped to 52 percent of the average white family income in 2000.

The 1991 CNBC theme was "Health, Wholeness, and Healing in the African-American Community: The Role of the Church, Part II." The church organizations included the National Missionary Baptist Convention of America, the African Methodist Episcopal Church, the Christian Methodist Episcopal Church, the Church of God in Christ, the National Baptist Convention of America, Inc., the National Baptist Convention, U.S.A., Inc., and the National Progressive Baptist Convention, Inc. For years, these historic institutions had tried to forge some common ground, if not unity. They at least needed to address effective joint solutions to black America's serious socioeconomic problems.

John Hurst Adams was founder of the CNBC effort. NMBCA officials F. Benjamin Davis and W.N. Daniel, who also served on the board of directors for the National Baptist Publishing Board, took leading roles in the 1991 CNBC meeting. The chairman of the National Baptist Publishing Board at the time was F. Benjamin Davis, who served as secretary of the CNBC board.

Given the new black Baptist realities, and with the approach of the 21st century, the National Baptist Publishing Board would have to consider making itself into a new kind of company and extending the customer base beyond what it traditionally had been. The National Baptist Publishing Board remained affiliated with the NMBCA, but also it was the prime publisher for other Baptist conventions by printing the Baptist hymnals, Vacation Bible School kits, Sunday school lessons, and other church needs. The *National Baptist Publishing Catalog* (1991) reached 94 pages and included children's books, books on counseling, marriage, and music, as well as traditional supplies for church and Sunday school. Boyd III instituted more company retreats and training sessions for the staff and workers. He invested heavily in modern equipment, including computers, color process printing, photocomposition machines, computer graphic software, micrographic equipment, and faster printing machines. He organized the company into five departments, including finance, publications, business development, marketing, and operations. The customer relations unit improved services and helped improve sales and collections. For the convenience of customers, the NBPB established distribution points through hundreds of religious bookstores. The company's on-site bookstore carried traditional items and the newest Christian publications.

As one of its historic anchors, the NBPB remained loyal to the National Missionary Baptist Convention of America. Even though the entire convention comprised less than 20 percent of the company's total revenues, the publishing house would contribute the largest percentage of its annual donations. At the NMBCA meeting in September 1993, some 10,000 people were reported in attendance in Cleveland, Ohio, where they addressed education, healthcare, gun violence, equal prosperity, and other issues for African Americans and Baptists. The theme was "The Church's Light Shining in a Darkened World." The delegates hoped the meeting would "bind [them] together to face any adversity and inform as many individuals as possible about the Word of God," according to Cleveland's *Call and Post* (September 9, 1993). Boyd III was there to address the audience regarding these issues. East Mt. Zion Baptist Church, under A. Charles Bowie, was the host church.

The NBPB's National Baptist Sunday Church School and B.T.U. Congress grew in size and significance. The 1992 Sunday School Congress session was held in Atlanta, where 25,000 people visited the event at the Georgia World Congress Center. The Atlanta Hilton Towers Hotel served as Congress headquarters. Messengers had a choice of 12 other hotels with special Congress room rates. The theme was "The Family: An Eternal Hope for Internal Crisis and External Conflicts" based on Nehemiah 4:13-15. The Morehouse School of Religion was the host, along with Hezekiah Benton; R.L. White, pastor of Mt. Ephraim Baptist Church; and Eddie Long, pastor of New Birth Baptist Church. Pre-registration was $30 and on-site registration was $35. The on-site class registration/enrollment was scheduled from Tuesday through Friday in the convention center. "To avoid the long lines at Congress and save money, take advantage of pre-registration," the *Union-Review* advised (January 1992). The intent was to keep the Congress as relaxed and convenient as possible, because for thousands of Baptists, this also was a week of vacation. Louis Sullivan, U.S. Secretary of Health and Human Services, and Joseph E. Lowery of the Southern Christian Leadership Conference were the main speakers.

The *Union-Review* (February 1993) printed the list of classes, registration forms, housing forms, hotel rates, advertisement rates for the *Souvenir Booklet*, and other pertinent information for the 1993 Annual Session of the National Baptist Sunday Church School and Baptist Training Union Congress, Detroit, Michigan, June 15-20,

1993. The theme was "God's Answer to Troubled Times," based on Jeremiah 31:13. *The Michigan Chronicle* (April 21, 1993) spread the word that the "Baptist Training Congress will address moral issues." Boyd III said that he believed that the solutions to the problem of moral decay in families and among our youth must start during childhood, which comes to be the responsibility of parents to teach children moral, social, and religious values. Some 30,000 people were expected to attend the week-long event and leave behind $10 million in the Detroit economy. Boyd and the Congress staff decided to add healthcare for African Americans as another major issue and invite the Michigan State Department of Health to do screenings for blood pressure, diabetes, and AIDS. All these diseases were killing African Americans at a faster rate than most other Americans who suffered the same ailments. Ministers were asked to take these health messages back to their churches.

Benjamin L. Hooks, the retiring head of the NAACP, was scheduled as the Thursday, June 17, speaker in Detroit. Entertainment attorney Gregory Reed spoke to the ministers. Barry Sanders of the Detroit Lions football team was the grand marshal for the parade, church drill teams were coming from across America, and some 3,000 participants were expected for the Congress parade. Youthful performers and speakers addressed the needs of the youth messengers. Oscar Alexis announced the 1993 Drill Team Competition and Rules in the *Union-Review* (June 1993). Even nationally famed gospel singers were scheduled to perform at the National Baptist Sunday Church School and B.T.U. Congress. The events were reported by the *Detroit Free Press* (June 18, 1993) and the *Detroit Monitor* (June 10, 17, 1993).

The erudite Reverend Jim Holley, Ph.D., a graduate of Tennessee State University and pastor of Detroit's historic Little Rock Missionary Baptist Church, which was founded in 1936, served as guest host. Dr. Holley said,

> It is our prayer that we will all be spiritually strengthened this week through the Congress activities, such as in the Christian education classes, general assemblies, meetings, oral and drill team competitions, and the overall joy that abounds when Christians come together. In your spare time, we encourage you to shop, go sightseeing, enjoy the fine food and the friendly atmosphere, or whatever it is you like to do. Enjoy your stay with us.

Mayor Coleman A. Young and Michigan Governor John Engler issued letters of welcome to Congress participants. Bobby Jones and New Life were the featured gospel artists for the pre-Congress musical at Cobo Hall Convention Center, along with a 500-voice mass choir. Dr. Charles G. Adams, pastor of Hartford Memorial Baptist Church in Detroit, addressed the audience on June 18. The Reverend Marvin Winans, an accomplished song writer and producer and the pastor of Detroit's Perfecting Church, addressed the Mini-Congress in God's Word and song. Winans started his church in 1989 with eight members, eventually claiming 1,800 members. Other speakers included Eddie Long of Atlanta and the pastor of Greater New Mount Moriah Baptist Church in Detroit. Dr. Holley's book, *An Exposition of Job: the Drama of Human Suffering* (NBPB, 1992) was presented, and he was available for book signings.

Holley's dynamic Little Rock Baptist Church, a beautiful neo-gothic structure in Detroit, with its vast congregation of all ages, included performing arts and outreach ministries, such as a food pantry, "Get Employed Today," Children in Progress (CHIP), Investment Club, Tree of Life Foundation Endowment Program, SWAT Evangelism, Jail Ministry, Mentoring and Tutoring, Candy Stripers (young nurses), Boy Scouts, Girl Scouts, Vacation Bible School, College Tours, Scholarship Ministry, Annual Easter Egg Hunt, "Heroes Night at the Park" (October), Thanksgiving Basket Program, Shoes for Children Program (December), and five Church choirs. Holley became the pastor on June 9, 1972. He and the congregation moved to its current location at 9000 Woodward Avenue in August 1978. A major renovation of the building's interior was completed in 1990.

During the 1993 Congress, Holley's church demonstrated a new enterprise, the Country Preacher Bakery, located across the street from the church. The purpose of the bakery was to be a money-raising ministry, involving ice cream and cookies, toward helping prospective college students realize their goal. Dr. Holley's host committee, congregation, and the City of Detroit facilitated such a good Congress that administrators returned the event to Detroit for the 2001 session. Two years later, Jim Holley had become the commencement speaker and Grand Marshall for the Homecoming Parade at his alma mater, Tennessee State University.

The *National Baptist Union-Review* (June 1994) previewed the National Baptist Congress at Columbus, Ohio. Edward Victor Hill (d. 2003), pastor of the Mt. Zion Missionary Baptist Church, one of the largest in California, was the keynote speaker. Hill was widely recognized as a Bible teacher, conference and convention speaker, and television evangelist. He served as pastor of Mt. Zion for more than thirty-three years, served as an officer in the NBC (USA), and belonged to more than fifty local and national organizations, including service as a trustee of Bishop and Morehouse colleges. To the Congress audience, Hill said, "I am pleased with the growth of this convention. The dedication of our members toward implementing the Word of God in finding solutions to the dilemmas facing congregations today is very uplifting." Friendship Baptist Church served as the host church. The pastor said: "This Congress, which will represent a very large portion of the membership of the National Missionary Baptist Convention of America, is looking forward to a week of uniting our spirits with one another and carrying out God's Word." Donald Washington organized a 300-voice mass choir, and Darrell Brooks was special guest musical artist. F. Benjamin Davis announced:

> The Congress tradition will be perpetuated...and we welcome such a splendid task...We need to continue to support Dr. Boyd and the National Baptist Publishing Board. The history has long been documented of their willingness and commitment to advance the kingdom of God while lifting the African-American church to a higher level.

Betty Seastrong of Antioch Missionary Baptist Church of Chicago said that one of the best, most basic resources of the National Baptist Sunday Church School and Baptist Training Union Congress has always been the personal, individualized input of the most active and concerned messengers to one of the most recognized Christian education institutions in the nation's community of religion.

Everyone could be a star at the Sunday School Congress, which, increasingly became a leadership academy. The NBPB invited "additional writers for Christian education literature and curriculum." The *Union-Review* featured "up-and-coming ministers," including Roderick C. Pounds Sr., pastor of Refuge Missionary Baptist Church in Ohio; Craig M. Smith, pastor of Metropolitan

Baptist Church in Chicago; and Bryant C. Wyatt, pastor of Mt. Calvary Missionary Baptist Church in Sacramento, California. The Publishing Board highlighted Beulah Stamps Lyons, who would celebrate her 100th birthday at the 1994 Congress. She had been a member of her church since 1935, as well as an officer and teacher. She held a college degree and honorary doctorate of humanities from a Baptist seminary. "God has been good to me . . . His gracious power in so many ways has blessed me through long years of happy days," she said. Mrs. O.B. Williams wrote from Portland, Oregon, to remind the national ministers' wives:

> Life can only be measured by the quality of love in it. Life can be seen as a celebration, a challenge, a journey and much more…Please remember at the Congress, we will be planning our outline of worship for our one-day session for the Convention in Dallas in September.

She had served six years as president of the ministers' wives, the *Union-Review* (June 1994) stated.

Again, a prime supporter of the Sunday School Congress was the East Mt. Zion Baptist Church (1908-present) of Cleveland, Ohio. A. Charles Bowie was the eighth pastor and had served for 17 years. Bowie was secretary-treasurer of the Evangelical Board of the National Missionary Baptist Convention of America. His ministry included youth, evangelism, outreach, visitation, music, transportation and teaching. Five hundred people attended the Sunday school classes each week, using NBPB literature. East Mt. Zion included one of the largest adult Sunday school departments in the region and an active Baptist Training Union. The church had several scholarship funds set aside to aid college students, as well as a 50-acre farm on which to develop a Christian camp.

The National Baptist Sunday Church School and B.T.U. Congress headed to Phoenix, Arizona, in 1995. In describing the impressive drill teams that dazzled the western city, the *Arizona Republic* (June 15, 1995) referred to the "young soldiers in God's military." The Congress was so successful, it would return to Phoenix within seven years.

In 1997, the Congress was held in Louisville, Kentucky, with Little Flock Baptist Church as host. About 20,000 people attended the week's events at the Commonwealth Convention Center. The city seemed impressed with the hundreds of youngsters reciting Bible passages at ease and in unison, according to the *Louisville Defender* (June 5, 1997). The Congress brought approximately $16 million to the Louisville area economy, the Louisville *Courier-Journal* reported (June 12, 1997).

The 1998 Congress was scheduled for Cincinnati, Ohio, June 7-12. The event remained the country's premier gathering of Christian education for adults and young people. Dr. A. Charles Bowie was scheduled to open the Sunday, June 7, services at the Inspirational Baptist Church. Other speakers included Kweisi Mfume, director of the NAACP, Henry K. Smith of Nashville's South Inglewood Baptist Church, and W.T. Snead, president of the NMBCA. Willie T. Snead was founding pastor of the Greater Temple of God Missionary Baptist Church in Los Angeles, established in July 1967, past moderator of the Pacific District Missionary Baptist Association of Los Angeles, and past president of the California Missionary Baptist State Convention. He held life membership in the NAACP. Dr. B.W. Noble was dean of the National Mini-Congress, which included liturgical dancing, a luncheon by Lane College, a talent hour, youth choir, B.T.U. activities, the T.B. Boyd, Jr. Oratorical Contest, drama presentations, drill team presentations, worship, singing, prayer, the Meharry Medical College Luncheon, the parade, Gospel Showcase, and the General Assembly.

At Cincinnati, T.B. Boyd III said, "This week we will be challenged to rediscover God's purpose for family life, His plan for the family's destiny, and His prescription for family dysfunction." The Congress' theme reminded the messengers, the family, as a "Divine Structure for Man's Destiny," had the responsibility of seeing the divine edicts of God are passed down to succeeding generations. From Nashville, Tennessee in 1906 to Cincinnati in 1998, the mission continued with the help of Almighty God and the encouragement of loyal supporters. The NBPB announced it was introducing four new books, three of which would be available at the Congress. The staff also announced the continuation of the annual March R.H. Boyd Memorial Week observation. Houston would be the host city on June 13-18, 1999, when 14 hotels, including the headquarters hotel, the Hyatt Regency, would be reserved. The 1999 theme was "The Family: A Bridge Between Heritage and Hope."

In 1999, Dr. Boyd extended an invitation for Quaford C. Coleman, a native of Los Angeles, to serve as General Assembly Coordinator for the National Baptist Sunday School Congress. He had served as a writer for the NBPB, an instructor at the annual Sunday School Congress, and the first Mini-Congress Coordinator. He served on the R.H. Boyd Family Endowment Fund committee and engaged many civic and religious endeavors in his home city. Coleman was in his 28th year as administrative assistant to Melvin V. Wade Sr., pastor of the Mt. Moriah Baptist Church in Los Angeles. Coleman helped gain a $4.5 million federal Housing and Urban Development grant to build a multistory complex for the elderly.

Boyd III was well recognized as a local and national leader. He was a charter member and the first president of the 100 Black Men of Middle Tennessee, Inc. He donated $100,000 to the organization, which nurtured young boys from elementary grades through high school (ages 10-17) and then gave them a scholarship through college. When the Second Annual Banquet for the 100 Black Men of Middle Tennessee was held, Boyd was the driving force behind the idea. On June 9-12, 1994, the Eighth Annual National Convention of the 100 Black Men of America was held in Nashville at the Opryland Hotel. Congressman Alcee Hastings, a graduate of Fisk University and a former federal judge, was the featured speaker. The convention theme was "The African-American Male: America's Conscience and Future."

Boyd and other members of the 100 Black Men of Middle Tennessee Chapter adopted Ross Elementary School, an impoverished public school, and promised to work in the school to improve retention and learning and put every boy in the program through college by providing for his tuition. Soon they were issuing $5,000 scholarships to several young men. T.B. Boyd III said,

> Children are our greatest asset and our most important investment. We must prioritize and make sure our children are our number one priority . . . We have no greater resource than our youth, no greater task than the orientation of molding of the young people," The *Nashville Pride* (August 4, 1995).

In 1996, Boyd III and the National Baptist Publishing Board received the Minority Trailblazer of the Year Award at the Minority Enterprise Development Week program.

Under the leadership of T.B. Boyd III and other family members, Citizens Bank weathered the financial storms, economic recessions, and depressions for nearly 100 years. Citizens Bank held a ribbon-cutting ceremony to celebrate the opening of the new branch in the new Kroger grocery store at the corner of 8th and Monroe Streets. This was Citizens' second branch, and it offered full service banking, where customers could stop by while shopping for groceries. Less than ten years later, Citizens would open another branch in Kroger on Clarksville Highway, while the main branch remained on Jefferson Street in the heart of the North Nashville shopping and college district. The administrative headquarters building for Citizens Bank was two blocks away on Heiman Street. When the National Bankers' Association met October 19-22, 1993, in Nashville, Boyd III and the president of Citizens Bank served as hosts to more than 200 bankers and corporate leaders and helped sponsor the prayer breakfast and golf tournament.

Citizens lost money under the different bank presidents between 1979 and 1995 ($245,000 in 1991 and $60,000 in 1994). Consequently, members of the board of directors hired another bank president, Deborah Scott-Ensley, a graduate of Tennessee State University and a current officer of the bank. Her basic philosophy of business was "honesty and good service." Ensley and Boyd led the bank's staff in turning things around, posting a 10.09 percent return on equity and a net income of $163,000 compared to the losses of the previous five years. The team evaluated expenses, accounts, and procedures and policies and expanded the bank's profits by expanding the Visa and MasterCard business to return the institution to its profitable days. "We evaluated also how we were pricing loans," said Ensley. She grew the commercial and industrial loans by 58 percent, while allowing consumer loans to shrink. In the *Nashville Banner* (March 23, 1995), Ensley said, "Our key focus as an organization is service; we cannot compete with those banks that are in places where we are not, but we can match services with anyone."

In the *American Banker* (February 18, 1997), Boyd III said, "Citizens Bank has built a business around lending money to minority businesses."

Boyd III and the Citizens Bank directors had taken a chance by breaking the "glass ceiling" in Nashville and appointing a female as bank president. However, Deborah Scott-Ensley, a bright thinker, was a perfect choice for the position. She completed an MBA and doctorate of education at Tennessee State University and earned further credentials at the Louisiana State University School of Banking and the Cannon Trust Operations School. By 2003, Citizens Bank could float loans of a million dollars or more under rules of the bank regulators, including the U.S. Comptroller of the Currency and the Federal Deposit Insurance Corporation. The institution was rated highly by these regulators, whose auditors found no fault in the bank's operations. By the 21st century, the bank's holdings were many millions of dollars beyond the imagination of the early founders. President Deborah Scott-Ensley said:

> There will always be a place for a well-run community bank. Operating an efficient and lean organization is the main key to surviving in this competitive business. There are customers who want personal service. So we will have super-huge banks, but we also need small community banks, like Citizens Bank.

Ensley became president of the National Bankers Association, which was founded in the early 1900s as an affiliate of the National Negro Business League, founded by Booker T. Washington, James C. Napier, and other leading "race men." The National Bankers Association had 57 members (Hispanic, Asian, African-American, and women-owned businesses) by 1997 with $31 billion in assets. Citizens Bank of Nashville was one of the few African-American banks remaining in the country. Citizens Bank began workshops at local churches, clubs, and other neighborhood organizations to better educate minorities on banking, loans, and home mortgages. Boyd III received special permission from the U.S. Comptroller of the Currency to serve on two bank boards at the same time.

Meanwhile, the National Baptist Publishing Board and the *Union-Review* proudly announced that staff writer Robert Churchwell was honored in April 1994 as a charter member of the Hall of Fame, Region VI of the National Association of Black Journalists. He completed Pearl High School in 1940, entered Fisk University, and served in the U.S. Army (1942-1945) before completing college and then graduating from Tennessee A&I State College. The college graduate wrote articles for the Nashville *Commentator* and joined the *Nashville Banner* staff in 1950 as its first Negro member. He had suffered the ordeal of having to submit his dispatches from home, and, when given a desk at the newspaper's office, Churchwell endured the racial slurs from other reporters. The head of the *Banner* fought against the sit-in demonstrations in 1960 and led the movement to get James M. Lawson expelled from Vanderbilt University's Divinity School in March 1960. Robert Churchwell endured his ordeal at the *Banner*, became a noted journalist, and eventually retired with dignity. He and his wife nurtured their children into college graduates, including two heart surgeons. Churchwell became a *Union-Review* staffer in October 1981, although he had covered NBPB events since Henry Allen Boyd's time.

The *Union-Review* (1994) lauded other great journalists and television personalities who got their start in Nashville. It pointed out Oprah Winfrey, a Tennessee State University graduate, who brought great honor to her alma mater. While a student at TSU, Winfrey became an anchor at Nashville's WTVF Channel 5 television in January 1974. She went on to Baltimore as news anchor in May 1976 and then to Chicago to became the talk show hostess on "A.M. Chicago," which became the nationally televised "Oprah Winfrey Show." She would return to Tennessee State University to receive a bachelor's degree in speech communications and was the commencement speaker 10 years after leaving for Boston. The "Oprah Winfrey Show" became the most popular talk show in America, reportedly making her one of the nation's billionaires. The *Union-Review* also paid homage to Bill Easley, the first Negro to become a staff member of the *Tennessean*. Other pioneers listed in the field included W.A. Reed, M.C. Chavis, W.F. Schackleford, Reginald Stuart, Teresa Harrison, Ester Fitzpatrick, Ann Holt, Dwight Lewis, Tam Gordon, R.H. Boyd, Henry Allen Boyd, T.B. Boyd, Jr., and T.B. Boyd III.

The NBPB and the *Union-Review* in 1994 also recognized the late Dr. Maud Anna Berry Smith Fuller, president of the Women's Auxiliary of the National Baptist Convention of America, 1927-1968. She and her husband owned a funeral home and burial association in Austin, Texas, until her death in 1971. She served as delegate to the Baptist World Alliance in 1939 and 1947. She made many trips to Africa to do mission work, and she was recognized on the national level for women's work. In 1944, she organized the youth department of the Women's Division of the National Baptist Convention of America. She was an untiring worker for the Lord, typical of many faithful women in the National Baptist Convention of America and within other organizations affiliated with the National Baptist Publishing Board.

On March 21-25, 1994, the National Baptist Publishing Board staff and employees celebrated "Rich Past, Exciting Present, Glorious Future" during R.H. Boyd Memorial Week at company headquarters. The broad emphasis of the exciting and educational week was on the substantial contributions to the nearly 100-year existence of the Publishing Board by each of its four top leaders, beginning with founder Rev. R.H. Boyd, whose leadership from 1896 to 1922 stands unmatched in the annals of African-American publishing of Christian education literature. The week included the official hanging of a montage portrait, showing four generations of leaders of the National Baptist Publishing Board, with a historic background of the old printing machines and buildings that served as a foundation for the company's history. The montage was hung on the walls of the sacred chapel in the NBPB's headquarters.

Of Richard Henry Boyd, the employees' historical tribute said, "We believe he prayed too, that God would help him prepare his successors so the work never would be interrupted." Of Henry Allen Boyd, the employees' tribute said, "Dr. Henry Allen Boyd loved to travel and speak. He was known all over the United States and in many foreign countries. He helped many churches financially. He got a joy out of helping those in need." Of T.B. Boyd, Jr., the employees' tribute said, "For those of us who were privileged to work for him, we sometimes worked beyond our own limits to produce work to evoke his praises." Of T.B. Boyd III the employees' tribute said, "We who work with him are always proud of him, and pray God will continue to be with him in all he and his great family strive to do in God's name for the National Baptist Publishing Board," according to the *Union-Review* (date unknown).

In November 1994, word arrived at the Publishing Board that one of its loyal supporters, Sylvester M. Wright of Dallas, Texas, had died. He was 64 years old and had suffered illness for some time.

Dr. Wright was known as a coalition builder and peacemaker in his community. He helped to calm racial strife in the 1960s. He said in 1988, "We fought hard to keep race riots out of Dallas." Some militants criticized S.M. Wright for his approach to race relations. Wright said:

> I was no downtown fellow. I was a black fellow fighting for my community, but how are you going to fight for your community if you don't know the decision makers?

S.M. Wright was born in Dallas on February 7, 1927, and joined the church in 1933. He finished Lincoln High School in 1944, served in the U.S. Army from 1945 until 1947, attended Bishop College (Marshall, Texas, founded 1881), and became pastor of Greater New Hope Baptist Church in 1951. He earned a master's degree from Bishop College in 1954. S.M. Wright was a natural leader, and, although born five years after R.H. Boyd's death, Wright was a loyal supporter of the legacy of R.H. Boyd. Wright became president of the Missionary Baptist General Convention of Texas in 1980. The Missionary Baptist General Convention of Texas celebrated its 90th Jubilee on October 17-21, 1984, under S.M. Wright. Reverends M.L. Price, Robert L. Rowe, G.W. Daniel, and Carlton J. Allen, as well as a 500-voice choir, assisted in the elaborate celebration in San Antonio. The choir appropriately sang a soulful rendition of "Lord, Help Me to Hold Out." Reverend Wright was in the forefront when the National Missionary Baptist Convention of America was formed. At the Palmer House Hotel and the McCormick Center, on September 9, 1989, when 8,000 delegates and visitors attended the musical for the new NBMCA, it was S.M. Wright who introduced Boyd III, calling him "my friend and our friend. He is one of our products." In 1993, S.M. Wright held the guiding role in the Human Relations Banquet of the Interdenominational Ministers Alliance of Dallas. Boyd III and E.V. Hill were among the invited guests at the banquet attended by thousands. Wright was elected president of the National Missionary Baptist Convention of America in 1994. The late S.M. Wright appeared irreplaceable. His two sons took over his church affairs and his legacy. The National Missionary Baptist Convention of America was then headed by the Reverend Willie

Snead, who was elected in September 1995, as reported by the *Tennessee Tribune* (September 8, 1995).

Boyd was still expending great energy and creativity in his various positions. He also was a member of the board of directors for First Union National Bank in Nashville and was March of Dimes' Man of the Year (1990). Besides being one of Nashville's "Best Dressed Men," he was a notable participant in local and national marathons, while also exercising and jogging daily in his neighborhood, one of Nashville's most prestigious places to live.

Again, operation of Citizens Bank required inordinate amounts of his time because a banking institution is heavily regulated by state and federal agencies and must be carefully attended to at all times. Not only were there monthly board of directors meetings, but there were a host of board committees in addition to meetings with the officers and staff of the bank, citizen advisory committee members, and customers who demanded attention from the chairman himself.

Church lending accounted for about 60 percent of the bank's loans. James Thomas, pastor of the prestigious Jefferson Street Missionary Baptist Church of Nashville, said, "When I could not obtain a loan anywhere else, I knew where to go. When I look at Citizens Bank, I see family. I see me," according to *Community Banking* (February 18, 1997). Thomas built a million dollar apartment complex near Tennessee State University with a Citizen Bank loan. In 1998, Citizens Bank of Nashville teamed with Citizen Trust Bank of Atlanta to loan Ebenezer Baptist Church $5.5 million to build a new sanctuary to house 2,000 members, according to *Nashville Urban Journal* (June 24, 1998). Citizens opened the Clarksville Highway branch in Kroger in the same month to serve 6,000 potential customers in Bordeaux and announced plans to reach out to Hispanics and other minorities, who were rapidly locating to Nashville-Davidson County. Citizens Bank teamed with the Fannie Mae Corporation to increase black home ownership because only 47 percent of African Americans owned homes, compared to 75 percent of white Americans, by 2002. Fannie Mae products allowed lower down payments on home purchases. Citizens Bank's assets grew from more than $36 million in 1997 to $46 million in 2002 and more than $53 million in 2004, as the institution headed toward the strategic goal of becoming a "$100 million plus bank." Despite all these activities, including the bank; the publishing board; the Sunday School Congress; his own home church, Mt. Olive Missionary Baptist Church on Albion Street; family matters; and civic and social activities, Dr. T.B. Boyd III continued to provide dynamic leadership in many other places.

Dr. T.B. Boyd III, President & CEO
of R.H. Boyd Publishing Corporation

Rev. W.N. Daniel and Antioch Baptist Church, Chicago

Dr. S.M. Lockridge

Dr. Nehemiah Davis

Dr. S.M. Wright and Family

National Missionary Baptist Convention of America Officers

CHAPTER EIGHT

T.B. Boyd III and Transformations of the National Baptist Publishing Board and R.H. Boyd Publishing Corporation

On June 10, 1996, the National Baptist Publishing Board held an elaborate banquet and a weeklong celebration for the "One Hundredth Anniversary Celebration" of the company—"A century of Publishing the Word and Lifting the Torch." Boyd, President and Chief Executive Officer, praised the Publishing Board's customers:

> Over the years, the Publishing Board has grown and prospered because of the support of Baptists across the country. You have not only encouraged and sustained us by purchasing our products, you have been steadfast in your friendship, and in the giving of wise advice and counsel when we needed it. For that, we are grateful. I am tremendously proud, yet humbled, to be at the helm of this historic institution as it begins its second century of publishing the Word and lifting the Torch.

The program included a professionally produced film of the company's history and heritage, and Benjamin L. Hooks was banquet speaker. Greetings arrived from President Bill Clinton, Vice-President Albert Gore, Jr., Governor of Tennessee Don Sundquist, Mayor of Nashville Phil Bredesen, Congressman of Tennessee Bob Clement, and other dignitaries. The audience sang "Lift Every Voice and Sing."

As part of the 100th celebration, the Publishing Board loaned its collection of art to display at the Carl Van Vechten Gallery at Fisk University. By gracing its publications with colorful art and illustrations since the early 1900s, the NBPB fed the customers' understanding and appreciation of the humanities as a method of interpreting Christianity. The artwork represented the brilliantly colored drawings that adorned the covers of Christian education publications through the years. The artists' renderings were done in watercolor, gauche', pen and ink, and colored pencil. The Publishing Board had used the renderings to depict the true essence of each Christian theme and subject within a certain magazine or other publication. Outside of the Publishing Board's customer base, the public was unaware of these outstanding, bold drawings that constituted a collection of Negro art resting in the archives at the National Baptist Publishing Board. According to Sterling Stuckey, *Going through the Storm: the Influence of African American Art in History* (1994), art is important to understanding the African-American experience in history.

In 1996, the NBPB reached 35,000 primarily African-American churches and laity with its annual catalog and quarterly publications. It also serviced more than 3,000 Christian bookstores. Today, the Publishing Board employs more than 200 writers, educators, technicians, and skilled trades people. It also employs professionals in the publishing, printing, and distribution of more than 14 million periodicals, books, pamphlets, hymnals, and newspapers across the United States and throughout the world. The company has remained a privately owned, not-for-profit religious publisher with annual sales of more than $10 million. It employs 140 permanent employees in a 55,000 square-foot printing plant and corporate headquarters. T.B. Boyd III has said:

> In a difficult time for the African-American man, Dr. Richard Henry Boyd had the faith to answer his calling. His courage and tenacity allowed him to fulfill his destiny—to publish the Word of God for His people . . . I stand on behalf of three generations who preceded me in leadership of the National Baptist Publishing Board to thank the great men and women who have, over the years, worked diligently for the success of this institution.—June 10, 1996.

Boyd III often could be heard at meetings, telling the employees, "There is no other company like this. It is the greatest corporation in the world." He praised them for engaging in the history of the company and keeping that history alive through annual pageants and programs, especially the annual R.H. Boyd Week program. The Company's Vision is:

> To continue as a great African-American corporation that will perpetuate the publishing, printing, and production of the highest quality of Christian literature and merchandise created in accordance with Baptist polity and sound business principles as inspired by God.

The Guiding Principles of the company are:

> Print, publish, and distribute Christian literature which confirms the full inclusion of all people into the miracle that is the birth, life, death, resurrection, and ascension of Jesus Christ; supply only resources and materials which uplift and encourage the church, the family, and the community.

The National Baptist Sunday School Congress ended the 20th century with its session in Fort Lauderdale, Florida, June 11-16, 2000. The sessions were held in the Convention Center, with the nearby Marriott serving as the headquarters hotel. Julian Bond, chairman of the NAACP, was the speaker for the event. Bill Campbell, who served 20 years in the Georgia legislature and as mayor of Atlanta, was a keynote speaker. The Mini-Congress, which was formed in 1979, constituted nearly 50 percent of the attendees; the event helped prepare them to be the Baptist leaders of the 21st century. A chaperoned orientation session was held to make sure the youngsters were well-behaved, exemplary Christians while in the hotels and on the streets of the host city. "The huge Baptist convention is a milestone for black tourism in the Fort Lauderdale area," said the president of the Ft. Lauderdale Convention and Visitors Bureau. Local citizens were amazed to learn African Americans made up 8 percent of travel spending, but spent as much as anyone else while on vacation. Some 25,000 messengers were expected to attend the events, including services at Mt. Calvary Baptist Church. The host pastor hoped "The event would make a difference in the community, both spiritually and economically," according to Fort Lauderdale's *Broward Times* (April 14, 2000). Boyd said the public was invited to attend the Congress sessions, according to the Fort Lauderdale *Westside Gazette* (April 27-May 3, 2000). The Baptist Congress dwarfed other meetings held at the 150,000 square-foot Broward County Convention Center, according to the *South Florida Sun-Sentinel* (June 11, 2000).

Finally, after 100 years of business, it was time to revamp the old NBPB and extend the programs, services, and materials to a new generation of customers. After four years of contemplation, study, and planning, the R.H. Boyd Publishing Corporation was established in the year 2000. A full-page advertisement in the *Tennessee Tribune* (July 18, 2000) touted the organization's accomplishment:

> R.H. Boyd Publishing Corporation, a global name in publishing for 100 years: a company with a vision of shaping the new millennium in Christian, educational, family, music, and historical publishing.

The company was named after the founder of the NBPB and was designed to publish and distribute hundreds of book titles in the areas of religion, family life, education, and history. The R.H. Boyd Publishing Corporation offered various national workshops and conferences in addition to traditional printing and publishing. The R.H. Boyd Publishing Corporation remained consistent in its commitment to produce the best Christian literature. The corporation also offered Christian educational services according to the needs of its clients, and educational ministries study opportunities. Contract work including book publishing, freelance writing, and graphic arts also were provided for the clients. The company's website says:

> As we step into the future, the R.H. Boyd Publishing Corporation will retain our posture as a national asset, having been a global name in publishing for over 100 years, spanning three centuries. We are more than a company . . . We're a tradition!

Besides T.B. Boyd III, President and CEO, the board members for the R.H. Boyd Corporation included F. Benjamin Davis (chairman), Nehemiah Davis (Texas), A. Charles Bowie (Ohio), B.W. Noble (Oklahoma), G. Thomas Turner (Ohio), and M.L. Jackson (Texas). The corporation included directors of the divisions of operations, publications, and marketing. Boyd III said the restructured entity provides greater business opportunities. "We are very excited about this new and exciting publishing venture," he said.

The new name shed some of the limited definitions and confusions in distinguishing the 100-year-old publishing house from its competitors. Boyd III had set some elaborate and ambitious plans for the R.H. Boyd Publishing Corporation. He intended to expand the company's writing staff and catalog offerings, explore construction of an additional office complex, keep up with rapidly changing technology, produce an electronic Bible for computer users, consider printing materials in several languages, and increasing international distribution of the products. Boyd said, "We thought there was no better time to make the announcement than during African-American History Month." The announcement appeared in the *Tennessean* (February 8, 2000) and the *Nashville Pride* (February 2000). The adoption of a new name did not mean the end of the road for the National Baptist Publishing Board. Boyd wanted to maintain the historical significance of what the company represented during its 100-year history. He had the NBPB remain an entity that continued to serve the church and the community by providing seminars, workshops, scholarships, endowments, and other donations to individuals and agencies benefitting society by promoting Christian values and good citizenship. The NBPB continues the mission of its founder through philanthropic contributions and activities.

Mable Louise (Landrum) Boyd passed away on May 19, 2001. Her sister, Reba Majors of Detroit, survived her, along with Mrs. Boyd's four children: T.B. III (Yvette) Boyd and children, T.B. IV, LaDonna, Shalae, and Justin; Margaret Jerrilyn Boyd-Hadley and child, Christopher; Brenda Joyce Boyd-Walker (John) and children, Ronald Wooding II, Jason, and Justin Walker; William Allen (Agnes) Boyd and children, Omari C., Yosef G., Oluwajare, and Zakiya; great-grandchild, Copper Boyd; two sisters-in-law; and a host of nieces, nephews, cousins, and friends. The funeral services were held on May 23 at her church, Mt. Olive Missionary Baptist Church on Albion Street. She was interred in the Woodlawn Mausoleum, where her late husband, T.B. Boyd, Jr., was laid to rest. The Reverend Marcel Kellar said in the eulogy, "Her love for her children was unconditional and without measure. She, like the mother in our narrative, will always be honored by her children."

The 2001 Sunday School Congress session would be held in Detroit's convention center and hosted by Dr. Holly of the Little Rock Baptist Church. The 2002 session was scheduled for Phoenix, Arizona. The 2002 theme was "Restoring the Word as Our Spiritual Foundation," based on Ephesians 2:19. Dr. Bernard Black, pastor of South Phoenix Baptist Church, was host pastor. Reverends Carl McDuffy and Rayford Johnson would serve as co-host pastors.

The *Union-Review* (May 2003) announced, "We're on our way to St. Louis!" The June 8-13, 2003, session was held at the Convention Center and messengers could register online. "Staying true to the founding mission requires a willingness to adapt and an ongoing effort to improve our educational offering," said Boyd III. Registration costs were $65-$80. The theme was "Changing the World, Using God's Word as Our Spiritual Foundation," based on Matthew 18:19-20. The agenda included classes and activities in the school of biblical studies, school of personal and spiritual growth, school of missionary education, school of ministry, and school of Christian teaching methodology; youth congress, youth activities, youth competitions and presentations, congress musical, and church dance ministry. Jim Holley, Gardner C. Taylor, Bernard Black, William Shaw, C.L. Rainey, Melvin Woodard, Calvin Butts, and David Groves, Ph.D. led the list of scheduled speakers. The opening church services were scheduled for Sunday, June 8, 2003, at West Side Missionary Baptist Church.

The 97th Sunday Church School Congress was hosted by Dr. Ronald Bobo, Sr., pastor of West Side Missionary Baptist Church. With moving words of spirit and in flaming tones of the Gospel, he eloquently said:

> It is with great joy and the love of Jesus Christ that I welcome each of you to the wonderful city of Saint Louis, Missouri for the 97th Annual Session of the National Baptist Sunday School and Baptist

Training Union Congress. I, along with the members of the West Side Missionary Baptist Church, extend to Dr. T.B. Boyd III, his staff, and all the messengers of this great Congress a hearty welcome! I anticipate the Lord is going to meet us this week in new and exciting ways! As you study the Word of God, I pray you will be filled afresh with the Spirit of the living God. I encourage you to join us as we "take this city for God." There are many who have no hope. Allow the Holy Spirit to use you as an instrument to share the hope of Jesus Christ with those you encounter this week. My prayer is for a Holy Spirit-led and a Holy Spirit-filled week of praise, worship, and study—all to the glory of our awesome, miracle-working God! To Him be all honor and praise!

Reflective of the Reverend Bobo and his standing in the community, the governor, mayor, aldermen, and district congressman sent letters of welcome to the Sunday School Congress. The Reverend Ronald Bobo operated a large traditional Baptist church. His ministry included the West Side Christian Academy, Excellence in Christian Education, pre-K through 5th grade, West Side Music Academy, West Side Federal Credit Union, West Side Food Pantry, substance abuse ministry, prison ministry, radio programs on KIRL AM Radio and KSTL AM Radio, and the regular Sunday, Wednesday, and Thursday services. In all his eloquence and wisdom, the Reverend Bobo concluded:

In this world of twists and turns, ups and downs, rights and wrongs, black and white . . . there is an answer. You may be at the top of your game; you may have struck out. You may be wonderfully in love. You may wonder what love has got to do with it. While you search for love, joy, and happiness, remember this: The God you have been looking for is looking for you. The life you've always wanted begins with a simple prayer. The purpose for which you were created is found in Jesus Christ. We believe He is the way, the truth, and the light. We offer this hope to you.

Dr. Melvin V. Wade, Sr. was the new president of the National Missionary Baptist Convention of America. He was assisted by officers C.C. Robertson, Bernard Black, Dezo McGill, C.E. Gaines, Robert Lee, A. Wayne Johnson, Walter Houston, W.R. Lott, Sr., T.L.

Brown, Aaron Brasfield, W.T. Burton, and L.C. Firle. President Wade said:

> Our National Baptist Sunday School and Baptist Training Union Congress sessions are designed to equip men, women, boys and girls for effective and godly leadership in the Church and community. Believers are called more than ever before to be trained servants who will become more spiritually vibrant, biblically strong, theologically balanced, Spirit-empowered, ministry-equipped, and culturally sensitive in order to be bold witnesses for God. I pray we take full advantage of this week.

In the nightly "Official Late Night Services" held in the headquarters Millennium Hotel, the display of young, dynamic ministers, pastors, and preachers undoubtedly showed the viability of the National Missionary Baptist Convention of America. The dynamic speakers included Cleophus Robinson, Jr., Mack McCollum, Kenneth B. Turner, Clay Evans, Charles Williams, L. W. Bolton, and others. Each night was standing room only, and services lasted beyond midnight. Despite the spread of new and unorthodox movements among many former Baptist churches in the African-American community, those who professed to be among the "biblically strong, theologically balanced, Spirit-empowered, ministry-equipped, and culturally sensitive" Baptist church continued the traditions, religious practices, and doctrines upon which their forefathers had built the foundations during the previous 230 years.

These young preachers' sermons would have been recognized in the American Baptist Missionary Convention of 1848, the sessions of the American National Baptist Convention in 1894, the slave brush arbors, and the old mill where the first Negro Baptist congregation began. The Silver Bluff Baptist Church met in the heart of "rice country" near Aiken, South Carolina, which was just across the river from Savannah, Georgia during the American Revolution (1770s). The "Old Landmark" preachers, like the late R.H. Boyd, would have been pleased that these young Baptist ministers at the Sunday School Congress were not ashamed to say, "I love the Lord." The Sunday School Congress and the NMBCA had helped to keep the African-American Baptist Church alive and pertinent.

At the end of the 2003 Sunday School Congress, T.B. Boyd III, officers, and friends left St. Louis for Indianapolis. Dr. F. Benjamin Davis, Chairman of the National Baptist Publishing Board/R.H. Boyd Publishing Corporation, had passed away. The funeral was postponed until the Saturday following the Sunday School Congress, so he could be honored for his long years of service to the Baptist denomination. He was recognized at the Sunday School Congress and throughout the African-American Baptist community for his leadership skills and Christian resoluteness. Davis, like the late W.N. Daniel, had taken T. B. III and nurtured, counseled, and protected him just as his father, T.B. Boyd, Jr., had requested on his death bed. Davis' loyalty and memories of Boyd, Jr. brought tears to the eyes of many. Dr. Nehemiah Davis preached the eulogy for Dr. Davis and stated that the name Benjamin means "unifier" or "son of my right hand" (Genesis 35:18). Dr. Melvin V. Wade Sr. said, "As I reflect on the life of Dr. Davis, I believe in sound biblical and fundamental Baptist orthodoxy." Funeral services were held Friday and Saturday, June 13 and 14, 2003, at New Bethel Missionary Baptist Church in Indianapolis, Ind.

F. Benjamin Davis was born May 19, 1912; and he earned bachelor's, master's, and doctorate degrees. He served as pastor of several churches, including New Bethel since 1954. F. Benjamin Davis served in many religious offices, including dean of the Sunday School Congress and chairman of the board for the NBPB/R.H. Boyd Publishing Corporation, regional vice-president for the Lott Carey Baptist Foreign Missionary Convention, regional vice-president of the Congress of National Black Churches, leadership in the Baptist World Alliance, and officer in the National Missionary Baptist Convention of America.

Because of the nurturing by F. Benjamin Davis and others, Boyd's stature as a leader at the Publishing Board continued to grow. He repeatedly earned a listing in *Who's Who in America*, including the 53rd edition (1999); the *Nashville Business Magazine* (April 2002) recognized him as No. 50 among "Nashville's 100 Most Powerful" (p. 30). They defined *power* as "the ability to effect and influence change and to be among the most elite of Nashville's people, regardless of color and race." In the article, Boyd said:

My general philosophy on life is that you must first learn about yourself. Realize your own potential and stretch your limitations. If you never forget where you come from, you can appreciate where you are while you dream about where you are going. This is the daily catalyst to what I do here at the Publishing Board.

When asked how he would like to be remembered, Boyd said:

I would like to be remembered as a man who appreciated all that life had to give. In other words, a man who put forth the best he could, hopefully to make a difference in someone's life that would be beneficial.

T.B. Boyd III was appointed to the Community Advisory Council of the Nashville Business Incubation Center in 2003, served on the Tennessee State University board for the TSU Foundation, and chaired the committee to study the feasibility to establish an African-American museum in Nashville. Francis Guess, who was a former Commissioner of Labor for the state of Tennessee and currently is director of the Danner Foundation of Shoney's, Inc., headed this effort. Guess was a "mover and shaker" in the financial community, and the first African American in modern times to hold a significant political position with the Republican Party of Tennessee. The prestigious magazine *Nashville Lifestyles* (October-November 2002) featured a profile of Dr. T.B. and Yvette Boyd III, noting their favorite restaurants and civic organizations. Yvette served on the board of the Gilda's Club of Nashville; Cheekwood Botanical Gardens; Fannie Battle Day Home; Girl Scouts; and the Ladies Hermitage Association, which owned, operated, and managed the Andrew Jackson Home. The magazine's June 2001 issue had featured a story titled "On Top of the World: Boyd Home," called La Shantin Vista, which overlooks Nashville. The home also was featured in *Unique Homes*. In 2003, a local publication listed Boyd number one among Nashville's "25 Most Influential African-American Leaders." The Boyd family and the Publishing Board often were featured in various journals and magazines, including *Nashville: A Pictorial History* (1981), G.R. Adams; *The African American History of Nashville, Tennessee, 1780-1930* (1999), B.L.

Lovett; *Nashville: City in Harmony—Photographs* (2002), Jacki Moss; and *Nashville Post: Real Estate Digest* (April 2003). The latter article ranked T.B. Boyd III as No. 42 among "Nashville's Most Powerful."

In 2003, the R.H. Boyd Publishing Corporation's catalog featured an expanded line of products and services. *The New 21st Century Hymnal* was offered in a loose-leaf edition and a pew Bible edition. The expanded products also included communion ware, new Bible selections, audio Bible, Bible software, church murals, backlit scenes for plays and church dramas, and hundreds of book titles. The expected traditional products, including *R.H. Boyd's Record Keeping System, Church Record and Roll Book, Teacher's Record Book,* and others, were continued in the new catalog. Besides the aforementioned Bible selections, the Bibles included audio, teen edition, large print, color study Bible, great print Bible, *Children's Illustrated Bible,* and more. There were items for Easter, Christmas, other religious holidays, and Christian coloring books for children. Also in the R.H. Boyd Publishing Corporation's catalog were books for parents, pastors, church leaders, families, counseling, and African-American history. There existed an entire series of books on church drill team competitions, rules, regulations, team devotional guides, and *Marching in Faith: Church Drill Team Instructional Video.* The catalog included a line of church, clergy, and choir robes; ribbons; badges; signs; T-shirts; and *Boyd's Sunday School Lesson Commentary* (2002-2003). The scholastic *Commentary* was designed to equip the teachers and edify students, "enabling both to increase their knowledge in the Word of God." The verse-by-verse format provides the best approach to preparation, presentation, and implementation of the Christian principles. "Its purpose is to reveal the will of God as we study the Word of God, so the reader might do the work of God." Additionally, the catalog included books, audio and video tapes, materials on personal growth, and management of individual and family life. The latest catalog was greatly improved over the *1984 National Baptist Catalog.*

In cooperation with the Metro area United Way organization, T.B. Boyd III established the R.H. Boyd Leadership Society in 2002 to help launch an initiative to recognize the unique value and contributions of African Americans' impact in their community. Membership in the R.H. Boyd Society was based upon annual giving to United Way of $1,000 and higher, and the project was a success. Dr. Boyd also served on the TSU Foundation Board and established a Boyd Family Scholarship at the university. He led the effort for the T.B. Boyd, Jr. Endowment Fund to donate $15,000 each to Fisk University and Tennessee State University. Boyd was co-chair of the Sixth Annual Meharry Circle of Friends Gala, which was designed to raise much-needed funds for Meharry Medical College's endowment fund and its students. He served as chairman of the citizens group to plan an African-American Museum for Nashville. On July 27, 2003, Boyd III was the chosen speaker for the Mt. Olive Missionary Baptist Church's Annual Men's Day Program. During the reception following the services, Boyd's home church thanked him for his contributions to the advancement of Christianity throughout the nation.

In the first decade of the 21st century, the legacy of R.H. Boyd and the Publishing Board is still alive within the R.H. Boyd Publishing Corporation. The National Missionary Baptist Convention of America is functioning strong. The Sunday Church School Congress is growing stronger and prospering; and the African-American Baptists, regardless of which Baptist convention their churches and pastors are affiliated with, if any at all, look to the 110-year-old National Baptist Publishing Board and R.H. Boyd Publishing Corporation as an institution of pride. Few other American corporations, regardless of color or origins, truly could say, "We are more than 100 years old, under homogenous leadership since our founding." Dr. Gardner Taylor, a keynote speaker at the 2003 Congress in St. Louis, Missouri said T.B. Boyd III was one of the leaders of "four generations of prominence" that guided the publishing house in Nashville. *Enterprise* magazine listed him as the eighth most influential person in the state of Tennessee, supporting the depiction of the family as one of continued prominence. The mantle placed on his shoulders in 1979 was a tough and heavy burden to bear.

Dr. F. Benjamin Davis, Chairman
National Baptist Publishing Board

The NBPB Sunday School Congress, 1988

Rev. Jim Holley, Ph.D.

Dr. Gregory Moss

Cadets and Dancers in Congress Parade, 2002

1. Addressing the National Baptist Sunday School and Baptist Training Union Congress in 2006.
2. 2006 Congress musical.
3. Choir performance at the 2004 Congress.
4. Family at the 2002 National Baptist Sunday School and Baptist Training Union Congress.
5. Congress speaker Ben Hooks, President of the NAACP
6. Drill Teams performing at the 2003 Congress.

1. 2002 Congress Parade
2. Dr. Gardner Taylor speaking at the 2006 Congress.
3. Dr. Joseph Lowery speaking at the 2006 Congress.
4. Dr. Forbes speaking at the 2006 Congress.
5. Little girl watching a 2006 Congress performance.

1. Senator Thelma Harper at the 2006 Congress.
2. Governor Phil Bredesen at the 2006 Congress.
3. Vice-Mayor Howard Gentry at the 2006 Congress.
4. Mayor Bill Purcell at the 2006 Congress.

1. Liturgical Dance Performance at the 2002 Congress.
2. Drill Team Performance at the 2002 Congress.
3. Congress Band Performance at the 2004 Congress.
4. Congress attendee moved by her experience in 2000.
5. Drill Team saluted by Dr. T.B. Boyd III at the 2002 Congress.

1. Shalaé Boyd, LaDonna Boyd, Justin Boyd and Mrs. Yvette Boyd.
2. R.H. Boyd Publishing Corporation printer.
3. R.H. Boyd Publishing Corporation bookstore.
4. The New National Baptist Hymnal 21st Century Edition.

The Epilogue

Forasmuch as many have taken in hand to set forth in order a declaration of those things which are most surely believed among us, even as they delivered them unto us, which from the beginning [they] were eyewitnesses and ministers of the word, it seemed good to me also, having had perfect understanding of all things from the very first, to write unto thee in order, most excellent Theophilus, that thou might know the certainty of those things, wherein thou has been instructed.
—Luke 1:1-4, KJV

Since 1896, the publishing house has operated continuously and successfully. The "Long Journey" has been tedious, treacherous at times, filled with pain, and joyous, often watered with the tears of the great ancestors, and then triumphant over the forces of opposition and darkness. Surely, the journey has not ended for the R.H. Boyd Publishing Corporation.

Toward the end of the 20th century and into the first decade of the 21st century, the business environment for black affairs in America became more complex. There were many national, state, and local Baptist associations in every region of the country. In Tennessee, for example, about 12 percent of African-American Baptists participated with the NBCA and with the state body—the Missionary Baptist State Convention of Tennessee. The latter Baptist agency had member churches that cooperated with the Middle Tennessee Baptist District Association. Several African-American Baptist churches joined white Baptist conventions including about 13 African-American Baptist churches. This also included First Baptist Capitol Hill in Nashville, it was affiliated with the more racially integrated American Baptist churches. A few churches affiliated with the Southern Baptist Convention issued an official apology for the SBC's past support of slavery and Jim Crow. Most African-American Baptist churches in Tennessee affiliated with the NBCI, supported the American Baptist College, the World Baptist Center headquarters and the Baptist Sunday School Publishing Board in Nashville. Fourteen churches in Tennessee were affiliated with the Progressive National Baptist Convention, Inc. The National Primitive Baptist Convention had about eighty-eight congregations and six associations in Tennessee. The Tennessee Regular Baptist Convention headquarters was located in Memphis. The Tennessee Baptist Missionary and Educational Convention, which supported LeMoyne-Owen College, had headquarters in Nashville. According to A.W. Wardin, Jr., *Tennessee Baptists: A Comprehensive History, 1779-1999* (1999), the black Old-Line Primitive Baptist Churches also were located in the state of Tennessee.

The African-American Baptist traditionalists faced threats other than the proliferation of the many black Baptist conventions. By the 1990s, many churches of the Southern Baptist Convention were bitterly divided by their controversy over fundamentalism. The conservatives continued to dominate the SBC, and the association remained relatively intact despite the annual disputes. The African-American Baptists, like the white churches, would be adversely affected by differences in theology, polity, and religious practices. These developments, particularly in the 1990s, effected the size of the black Baptist membership and the business concerns of the religious publishing industry. In an environment where church membership was declining, black churches and their membership strength became adversely affected by the younger generation of African Americans. This generation shunned the same traditional Baptist services that had attracted and sustained the spirits of their parents, grandparents, and great-grandparents.

The establishment of the Full Gospel Baptist Church Fellowship began to attract many of the youth from the traditional African-American Baptist churches. Young preachers in the Full Gospel movement sometimes gained control of traditional Baptist churches from within and converted members into the Full Gospel fellowship. Others simply deleted the word "Baptist" from the name and called the place a general term such as "The Community Church" in order to attract non-denominational worshipers. The Full Gospel churches with their young, business-oriented ministers emphasized a cross breed of Baptist and Pentecostal theology, including the Holy Spirit, speaking in tongues, capitalizing on there being more women and youth in the ministry, and emphasizing spiritual and economic uplift. Often these congregations, especially in Atlanta, Memphis, Nashville, and New Orleans attracted large groups of high school and college students. Several of them became mega-congregations, with thousands of members and huge budgets that enriched ministers and others in the congregation.

The Full Gospel Baptist ministers dazzled the crowd in their special cut robes and expensive suits. They preferred to be called Bishop, which the Church of God in Christ has used for decades in its centralized Episcopal governing structure. A few former preachers of the COGIC started the movement in the Memphis area in the early 1990s, often holding the Full Gospel conventions at the Golden Gate Full Gospel Baptist Church. Memphis is the headquarters for the Church of God in Christ, which had split from the Holiness churches almost a hundred years ago. The Full Gospel Baptist Church Fellowship would have thousands of members and dozens of churches. Court battles about attempts to use Church of God in Christ names, traditions, and symbols also emerged. The small traditional Baptist churches and the young people, who often were not trained in Baptist doctrine and theology, but who also needed a God that was relevant, were easily attracted to the Full Gospel Baptist movement.

Perhaps the officers of the R.H. Boyd Publishing Corporation were wise and farsighted in transforming the company to meet the challenges of the 21st century business environment. The national economy was fast becoming a global economy with producers, consumers, workers, and customers separated by thousands of miles of land and sea, and yet tied together by the Internet, telephone lines, fax machines, and satellite communications. The R.H. Boyd Publishing Corporation would have to retain as much of its traditional customer base as possible, but the 21st century company also would have to seek out new worlds and new customers, and look into the global market. There were endless opportunities to do business with a diverse clientele in various places in the east and west.

On January 24-28, 2005, the four major national black Baptist conventions held a historic joint Winter Board Meeting in Nashville, Tennessee, at Gaylord Opryland Hotel. The event was attended by an estimated 10,000 delegates, messengers, and visitors mainly representing the four major National Baptist associations for African Americans. Since John Hurst Adams and others established the Annual Consultation of Councils of National Black Churches a decade and half ago, this was the first attempt to hold a meeting of African-American Baptists with the possibility of unifying them into one common set of purposes, if not one organization. Nashville was the proper place for the unity meeting, because the city was headquarters to several African-American religious conventions, three black religious publishing houses, and the site of religious and unity meetings since 1867. Although there was enthusiasm and optimism at the Opryland meeting, these tasks seemed nearly impossible given the tumultuous history of disunity among America's African-American Baptists.

In 1848, free northern Negroes incorporated the first national Negro Baptist Convention as the American Baptist Missionary Convention (ABMC). But once 90 percent of Negroes became free during the Civil War, disputes over governance split the black Baptists into several regional conventions by 1866. However, a merger was carried out amongst these regional conventions and the Consolidated American Baptist Convention (CABMC) held its first meeting in Nashville in August 1867. In 1873, the CABMC split again over regional issues, and in 1879 this national Baptist organization dissolved itself. Some black Baptists formed the Baptist Foreign Mission Convention in 1880 to do work in Africa. Black Baptists met in St. Louis in 1886 and formed the American National Baptist Convention (ANBC). Although they tried to make this organization embrace all Negro Baptists, during a merger meeting in Nashville in 1888, the Baptist General Association of the Western States and Territories refused to cooperate. In 1892, the Negro Baptists formed a third organization, the Baptist Educational Convention (BEC).

Finally, on September 28, 1895, the three large organizations (BEC, ANBC, and the Baptist Foreign Mission Convention) met in Atlanta and merged into the National Baptist Convention, U.S.A.

This merger lasted until September 1915, when the dispute over governance (incorporation and centralization) and ownership of the separately chartered boards, including especially the National Baptist Publishing Board, exploded into a bitter division and the creation of two national conventions: (1) The National Baptist Convention of America (NBCA), which preferred an unincorporated association governance and the autonomy of the NBPB under R.H. Boyd; and (2) the National Baptist Convention, U.S.A., Incorporated (NBCI), which proceeded to force the boards to surrender their individual charters and submit to national convention control. Over the next six years, attempts by the NBCI to gain control of the NBPB through the courts failed, and so did efforts by the Southern Baptist Convention to get the two Negro conventions to reunite. The Lott Carey Foreign Mission Convention, which embraced churches in Virginia and other eastern places, remained independent since its formation in the 1890s.

During disputes over the Civil Rights Movement and debates about how much the black church should be involved in this critical movement and whether the NBCI should support Martin Luther King, Jr. and other civil rights leaders who used civil disobedience tactics; the National Baptist Convention, U.S.A., Inc. engaged a violent split. This resulted in the formation of yet a third large national black Baptist association, the Progressive National Baptist Convention, Inc. (NPBC).

In 1988, the National Baptist Convention of America underwent a split in dispute of governance (incorporation), the Sunday School Congress, and control of the constituent boards particularly the National Baptist Publishing Board. As a result of this latter division, the National Missionary Baptist Convention of America (NMBCA) was chartered, this affiliated NBPB with the NMBCA.

On paper, these denominational divisions led to the creation of additional publishing house ventures. However, with inadequate capital to form such businesses in a highly competitive, technological printing and publishing market in the late 20th and early 21st centuries, the new black Baptist publishing had troubling concerns such as no plants, little or inexperienced staff, and owned or leased outdated facilities. Issues such as these were important because these commodities were needed in order for publishing houses to be competitive in America's fast evolving capitalist economy. Often, their work was sent to white owned printing and publishing companies. As a result, the better capitalized and more technological white printers and publishers divided up much of the black church printing business. However, the modern NBPB and R.H. Boyd Publishing Corporation kept blacks in the technology game.

T.B. Boyd III became involved in helping to convene the Baptist conventions in Nashville, Tennessee, a logical place for the meeting. The Nashville convention bureau and the Chamber of Commerce were brought on board, and the city's government sent letters of invitation. Leaders were brought in to tour the Opryland Hotel complex, which had thousands of rooms for guests, meetings, banquets, and acres of trees, water falls, and walkways under one roof.

By the time the unity convention convened in Nashville in January 2005, not only was there a black Baptist community in need of revival and unification, but there were at least four national conventions representing African Americans: (1) National Baptist Convention of America, Inc.; (2) National Missionary Baptist Convention of America; (3) National Baptist Convention, U.S.A., Inc.; and (4) the Progressive National Baptist Convention, Inc. Additionally, as aforementioned, including the Primitive Baptists, the Full Gospel Movement, Lott Cary Foreign Mission Convention, and others, the African-American Protestants were as varied and in as much disarray as the white American Christians and their many conventions. There were millions of black Baptists, and some charismatic clergymen often claiming to be Baptists (at least in the first instance) seemed to be taking advantage of these easy pickings.

When the unity delegates convened in Nashville, the "State of the African-American Community" was not a bright one, but it was far from hopeless. Indubitably, the black church could not afford to be in disunion. Nearly 28 percent of African Americans were stuck in poverty—a generation since President Lyndon Baines Johnson's War on Poverty. Some 140 years since slavery, neither the black church, nor lay black leaders, or the masses of blacks had figured out how to gain socioeconomic parity with other Americans. Besides the rapidly declining health of African Americans, sexually transmitted diseases, hypertension, diabetes, heart disease, obesity, infant mortality, short life expectancy rates for adults, drug and alcohol addiction, and death from homicide were at higher rates than other Americans. There are major problems facing America's black community. Some of the major ones are listed below.

(1) More young black youngsters were coming from weak, non-traditional family structures. The two-head household African- American family had deteriorated to only 38 percent by 2005, whereas in 1950, nearly 70 percent of Negro families had two-head households. Single-headed households had half the income of two-head families. Therefore, the black family had less money to properly educate the children, and fewer adults to give discipline in the home for the children. The weakened black family's median income and wealth had sunk below that of Hispanics, who had a higher median family income than blacks by 2005. The median income for black families overall was 37 percent less than the median income for the average white family; and black families at all income levels held much less average wealth than white American families. For sure, there were isolated spots of riches in the African-American community (among professional athletes, entertainers, businessmen, and even illegal industries). But in America's black community, about five generations since slavery, there is not any wealth. This is because of the inability to pass on huge sums of land, money, businesses, trust funds, stocks, bonds, banking institutions, and other lasting assets to future generations.

(2) Black church membership began to stagnate as members became older, and youngsters either stopped attending churches (although at a slower rate than white youngsters), or they began to be attracted by the glamour of the mega-churches with the animated services, the big choir sound, and the parking lots filled with shiny cars. Ministers of many of these congregations wanted to be bishops or archbishops, complete with the pageantry and regalia of the medieval church. The black youngsters were confused because they were lacking a base in religious philosophy and they were deprived of the church doctrine. Nevertheless, the big churches entertained the youngsters, while the traditional black church remained without common and unified purposes, void of truly modernized programs, and lacking the strategic plans needed to win and retain the hearts, souls, and loyalty of the young people.

(3) As poverty set deeper into the black community, newfound black political power failed its promises to deliver the spoils of victory. Despite the tremendous increases in black political influence soon after the Voting Rights Act of 1965, African-American politicians seemed to have lost sight of the goals of the civil rights movement. Black politicians also began to seek personal riches before pursuing group goals such as the reformation of health care, improving employment, and increasing black businesses that would create jobs for African Americans. Blacks had billions in total gross national product, but the number of black banks, for example, had shriveled from forty-two or so at the first quarter of the 20th century to a mere twelve of the nation's 59 minority banks by 2005. Nashville's Citizens Bank was celebrating its 101st birthday as the oldest continuously owned and operated black bank in America. On the other hand, many large black communities, such as St. Louis, no longer had a black owned bank; and the one in Richmond, Virginia, was months away from being sold to white investors. The splintering of the black religious community, as well as the general disunity among black American leaders, furthermore, allowed other banks, businesses, printing; and publishing houses to siphon off great portions of the black gross national product. This economically debilitating process disallowed African Americans the capital funds needed to tackle social problems, improve healthcare in the communities, build and sustain a productive political economy that would finally allow the African Americans to become equal American citizens.

(4) A huge influx of immigrants and other minorities were diverting the nation's attention away from focus on African Americans and their social and economic problems. By 2005, more Africans were entering America each year than during the slave trade. The new African immigrants were Muslim and/or Catholic. These African immigrants preferred to establish their own Christian churches instead of fusing with African-American religious culture. Seldom did they affiliate with established churches of the African Americans, who had their own internal church problems. When the black church began to recede in influence in its own community, the federal administrations instituted a policy of "benign neglect" that increasingly ignored the weakened African-

American community, which by 2005, no longer constituted America's largest minority community. Blacks comprised 12.4 percent of the American population, but Hispanics constituted about 14 percent, and Asians were growing faster than any group.

(5) Except for the bulldog tenacity of the NAACP, most lay and religious leaders and lawyers in the black community, had backed off from insisting on quality education since *Brown v. Board of Education* (1954). Apparently, these complacent men and women were unaware of the need for them to be proactive as church leaders, political, legal, and civic leaders in supporting the public schools and colleges. These institutions serviced their future—the youngsters. Yet, an entire generation of black youngsters seemed trapped in poorly performing resegregated schools in the largest cities, while the authorities looked the other way. African Americans were the only group to relinquish the teaching, learning, and training of their young to other ethnic group teachers. Less than 10 percent of the nation's teachers were blacks, but minorities constituted nearly 40 percent of the public school students. On average, less than 40 percent of African-American high school graduates enrolled in college compared to 46 percent of white high school graduates in 2001. About 1.8 million blacks were among America's nearly sixteen million college students by 2001, but most black college students were enrolled in junior colleges, where less than 25 percent of them graduated with an associate (2-year) degree.

(6) The historically black colleges and universities were still the mainstay of black higher education and training in the United States, but black leaders seemed not to be paying much attention to these HBCUs. The number of black colleges had decreased from about 128 in the 1920s to 106 by 1954, and to only 103 by the year 2000. Since the opening of the 21st century, three black colleges (all with religious affiliation)—Morris Brown College, Knoxville College, Edward Waters College had lost accreditation, and soon could close for good. As one philosopher said, "Every man's death diminishes me." And so, too, the death of a black college diminished the potential of all African Americans. The 103 historically black colleges and universities (HBCUs) constituted only 3 percent of the nation's nearly 4,000 colleges and universities; but, the HBCUs enrolled nearly 300,000 (16.7 percent) of the 1.8 million

black college students in 2001. More importantly, most students
enrolled at the HBCUs were in four-year college programs and not
junior college programs as they were in the white institutions. The
HBCUs graduated 25 to 30 percent of all black college students in
the nation. At the traditionally white (including junior, city, techni-
cal, and community) colleges, where 83 percent of the black college
students were enrolled by 2002, the graduation classes averaged
about 12 percent blacks. Graduates from the HBCUs earned more
money, had higher leadership aspirations, and were more likely to
attend graduate and professional schools than blacks who graduated from the white colleges and universities. Most of America's
African-American engineers, physicians, dentists, teachers,
lawyers, military officers, and other black professionals were products of HBCUs. By 2003, these minority institutions still were listed
among the top ten institutions as baccalaureate-institutions-of-ori-
gin for African Americans who completed Ph.D. degrees in
engineering, mathematics, and other sciences.

Because of the lower income and less wealth in the black families,
a higher percentage of black college students depended on financial
assistance, especially high interest loans. Whereas the HBCUs averaged 80 percent black students (20 percent were whites and others),
had to deal with financial aid in greater proportion, these minority
institutions buckled under the financial burden compared to white
four-year colleges and universities. The African-American community was not sending massive support to the black colleges to help
with scholarships and fellowships. Yet, a quarter of the HBCUs had
less than $6 million in endowment funds by 2001, and one small
HBCU had less than $445,000 endowment. Harvard University had
$24,000,000,000 and Vanderbilt University had $2,500,000,000 in
endowment funds, for example, while the largest endowment
among HBCUs was Howard University with under $350,000,000
endowment fund by 2004.

(7) The states and the federal government were spending more
money on prisons, which held a shocking 25 percent of the world's
imprisoned population. About half of America's prisoners were
blacks, Hispanics, and other people of color, mostly with poverty
backgrounds. In Tennessee, blacks comprised 16 percent of the
state's population but more than half of prisoners. The statistics

were similar or worse in areas with heavy black populations, especially in the nineteen former Jim Crow states. Often, blacks were the victims caught on the nation's highways according to federal reports (2001), in "sting operations," and in federal, state, and local coordinated raids in the minority communities. Policemen, state patrol officers, and federal agents could earn bonuses and rewards (just like slavery times) for allegedly confiscating illegal substances and apprehending alleged criminals, allowing many of the officers to retire early and enriched. The whites in the suburbs, small towns, and the cities comprised the majority of drug transporters, drug brokers, blue-collar criminals, and especially the users of expensive drugs (i.e., cocaine and heroine), but seldom did they go to jail or serve cruel and unjust long prison terms for the same crimes committed by minorities. A slave was worth $1,250 in 1860; but in 2004 a black prisoner was worth up to $26,000 a year to state appropriations that passed on to private prison companies. Blacks and other citizens paid the bill, while the wealthy and the conservatives had found another way to siphon off much needed public funds. The nation's profitable prison system was privatized including stockholders among leading politicians and America's elite class who earned a big return of interest and dividends with guarantees on some state prison contracts [i.e., Tennessee] of no more than 5 percent vacancy rate in prison beds. To maximize profits, the correction companies withheld behind-the-walls college education to the prisoners, and did little to rehabilitate them. No surprise that over 70 percent of those released from prison returned there, to further enrich American and foreign stockholders in the private corrections corporations. Additionally, America's profitable prison system was located in small towns; this provided jobs for whites and sustained their local economy. Again, American jails, prisons, penal farms, and juvenile facilities held 25 percent of all the civilian prisoners in the whole world. Nevertheless, few black and minority leaders, not even the church leaders, were complaining—as if they were unaware of the immoral, corrupted American criminal justice process and the "high tech slave catching system" existing in the twenty-first century.

All the above dynamic factors, corrupted processes, and historical events caused the four black Baptist conventions to convene in

Nashville in 2005 in a unity meeting. And all this unity business was reflective of the history of the 1890s and early 20th century, when the Negro Baptists were forced to come together to survive the awesome march of Jim Crow, white supremacy, and their intentional destruction of the socioeconomic progress and social competitiveness of Afro-Americans. And because blacks had chosen to forget that tragic history, or voluntarily decided to "suffer historical amnesia" that Fredrick Douglass in 1895 had warned against, African Americans were condemned to repeat that unfortunate history. Therefore, a hundred years or so after 1895, the African-American Baptist leaders again were pressured to unify their resources because of awesome, destructive external forces, as well as their own Christian desire to help solve the problems. It was really in their best interest to do so.

The leaders of the largest of the black Baptist conventions in 2005 were (1) Major L. Jemison, president of the Progressive National Baptist Convention, Incorporated; (2) William J. Shaw, president of the National Baptist Convention, U.S.A., Incorporated; (3) Stephen J. Thurston, president of the National Baptist Convention of America, Incorporated; and (4) Melvin V. Wade, Sr., president of the National Missionary Baptist Convention of America. The unity meeting held in Nashville in January 2005, was truly historic. Unfortunately, it was inconclusive.

Although some of these conventions claimed greater membership than others, there never was real statistical research to back up the claims. At any rate, the financial income of none of them reflected the inflated membership numbers. Nevertheless, without fiddling with estimated budgets, the four conventions vowed at the Nashville unity meeting in 2005 to launch collaborative ventures to address same-sex marriage, the relationship between church and state, and issues of racism, discrimination, and black economic empowerment. Indeed, these learned men and women were well aware of the problems and issues they faced in America. The final forum held on Thursday, January 27, was titled "African-American Perspectives [Solutions] on Economic Development and Political Empowerment." Julius Scruggs of the NBCI said, "The African-American church possesses that power to shape public polity, become supporters of Christian education, and use their resources to keep the doors of black colleges open." The four conventions held separate meetings on Friday.

A highlight of the Joint Winter Board Meeting was made by T.B. Boyd III, CEO and President of the National Baptist Publishing Board, R.H. Boyd Publishing Corporation, and chairman of the board of directors of Citizens Bank. He stated to the audience on Monday night, "When we join together, we can do anything." There seemed to be a lot of tension in the air on the first night of the meeting. When Boyd waited to be called to the microphone, he "could feel the need to relieve the tension not only among the people on the stage but the audience as well." So, once at the podium, he said, "Turn to each person on the side of you, and say 'God loves you; and God knows I'm trying.'" The crowd broke into laughter and joy, as members of the audience turned to each other with these greetings. When the meeting began, most of the tables were occupied by persons from the same denomination and churches, but Boyd's humorous gesture forced them to reach out and interact with one another, even from one table to another. The tension was broken; the atmosphere now was relaxed; and, a sense of being there for one purpose, unity of black Baptists, became a reality. This seemed to help set the tone for the rest of the week for the Joint Mid-Winter Board Meeting.

Ironically, the NBPB had been opposed by some of these groups since 1915; but, the 109-year-old publishing house was the strongest African-American corporation owned and operated wholly by blacks and remaining among the 21st century black Baptists after all the decades of dispute and disunity. Dr. T.B. Boyd III announced to the cheers of the audience that the $30,000 costs for printing the *Souvenir Booklet* was a donation to the unity meeting. After communicating with the four denominational presidents since October 2004, Dr. Boyd had sent a letter (January 3, 2005) to the National Baptist Press, Inc. of the NBCA in Shreveport, Louisiana, saying the R.H. Boyd Publishing Corporation was submitting "a bill on the printing of the Joint Winter Board Program; however as a courtesy to the conventions we will complete this project at no cost." This was no easy task, because the booklet ended up being 240 pages of color and black and white requiring the pulling together of an extensive amount of information, photographs, and designs into a comprehensive and orderly publication. Boyd presented a complimentary hard copy *Souvenir Booklet* to each of the four presidents. The R.H. Boyd Publishing Corporation also had worked with the Baptist Sunday School Board, also located in Nashville, to produce the various publications for the Joint Winter Board Meeting. President Boyd and the publishing house continued the 109-year-old tradition of insisting on "first-class, quality work," similar to the Reverend Richard Henry Boyd's 1917 pronouncement:

> We make everything from a post card to an encyclopedia and from a calling card to a Bible. Our literature is written by Negroes, set upon linotype machines owned and operated by Negroes, printed on printing presses owned and operated by Negroes, finished in a book binding plant owned and operated by Negroes, and sent out for use by Negro Baptists.

Things were somewhat changed in the technological age, but the R.H. Boyd Publishing Corporation and the non-profit National Baptist Publishing House, yet operated upon the R.H. Boyd philosophy of uplifting African Americans to be equal in printing and publishing with other Americans.

Dr. T.B. Boyd III and the R.H. Boyd Publishing Corporation sent an additional nine copies of the *Souvenir Booklet* (hard cover) to each of the four denominational presidents. The Publishing Board's *Union-Review* (February 2005), publication that is about a hundred years old, proclaimed "Joint Winter Board Meeting, a Tremendous Success." In the *Souvenir Booklet*, Pastor E. Boyd Esters of Community Missionary Baptist Church of Compton, California, said, "This important spiritual gathering invites us to share our love of Christ, to share our sense of mission and to share our love one for another. Our survival is linked to our oneness in the Lord."—the *Souvenir Booklet* (p. 194).

Some observers in that Opryland meeting hall including the author of this book, had to wonder: How many persons present at the unity meeting in Nashville, 2005, were really committed to a unification of the African-American Baptist conventions into one organization and the development of a truly national African-American agenda? How many of them were mere spectators? Could they give unconditional support to their existing thriving black Baptist businesses and create a true black political economy that uplifts all African Americans such as Dr. R.H. Boyd, Booker T. Washington, W.E.B. DuBois, and other progressive leaders strived to do in the period 1896-1915? At the end of the week, in the year 2005, it seemed most of them were willing and able to try.

— Bobby L. Lovett (March 26, 2005)

▲ Boyd Christmas, 2003

▲ The R.H. Boyd Publishing Corporation,
6717 Centennial Boulevard
Nashville, TN

National Missionary Baptist
Convention of America,
1988

◀ Yvette Boyd

▼ First Class Mailing Department

◀ The NBPB and
NMBCA
Sunday School
Congress

▲ Company Brochures

Appendices

APPENDIX A

MANSIONS SYMBOLIZED SUCCESS OF EX-SLAVE, DESCENDANTS
George Zepp, *The Tennessean*

As young boys in the early 1940s, my friends and I would pass on walks an impressive mansion that took up half a city block at 16th Avenue North and Heiman Street.

A shiny black limo with an open seat in front for a chauffeur and a closed back for passengers sat under an attached portico.

Older people later told me it was built by the Boyd family, founders of the black Citizens Savings Bank, one of two mansions built by the Boyds. The other was at 16th Avenue and Meharry Boulevard.

Did the one at 16th and Heiman burn down or what did happen to it? – Everette Morris, Nashville.

The two homes—one still standing, the other now gone—were evidence of the vision and success of an ex-slave and his Nashville descendants.

Richard Henry Boyd moved here from Texas, making his fortune meeting the spiritual and banking needs of African Americans in Nashville and elsewhere.

Boyd's National Baptist Publishing Board, started in 1896 to supply literature to black churches, and the Citizens Savings Bank and Trust he headed here were revolutionary for an oppressed minority.

But Boyd's interests were vast. He started a newspaper, The Globe, to give a strong voice to a growing segment of Nashville's population. He helped form the Nashville Negro Board of Trade and even began a doll-manufacturing company to make sure black children had toys with a positive image.

His early years after his 1843 birth into slavery in Mississippi included aid to his Confederate masters during Civil War fighting and a period in Texas as a cowboy and a preacher. Boyd began to realize black Baptist Sunday schools in his Texas district and elsewhere lacked teaching materials.

San Antonio, where he lived at the time, wasn't well suited to such a venture because of its location, Boyd believed. Relocating to Nashville in 1896, he founded the publishing firm by the end of that same year while living in a boarding house here.

"Boyd telephoned his son, Henry Allen, and directed him to ship a typewriter and two quilts from San Antonio," Tennessee State University historian Bobby L. Lovett wrote. The venture, marketing literature to churches across the country, proved vastly successful.

Just four years later, in January 1901, the Nashville American newspaper featured him in an article headed "How a Colored Man Started Publishing Housing in Nashville and Made a Fortune." By then he was employing 107 workers.

The year before he died in 1922, in his house at 1602 Heiman St., Boyd's company was printing 7.5 million periodicals. The figure was down from 11.7 million in 1909, due in part to the economy and an influenza outbreak.

His son, Henry Allen Boyd (1876-1959), later took on the father's role in most of the family endeavors. The son became secretary-treasurer of the National Baptist Publishing Board, president of the bank and editor of The Globe.

It was Henry A. Boyd who built the two-story brick house at 1603 Meharry Blvd., now a restored element of the Fisk University campus.

"He built it for his wife, a Fisk alumna, because she wanted to be close to the campus," said Reavis Mitchell, historian at Fisk.

The house, on what was in earlier times called Harding Street, continued as Henry A. Boyd's until he gave it to the university. City directories show he moved into the Heiman Street residence that had formerly been his father's by 1942.

The city directory that same year lists 1603 as a senior girls' "Boyd House" had served over the years as a men's dorm, a guesthouse and as home of the university's Honors Program. It was among the structures supporting the university's 1978 listing on the National Register of Historic Places.

The house had fallen into disrepair by 1993, but a lease arrangement with a dentist and her husband who hoped to restore it offered one possibility. However, the finding of asbestos inside and removal costs became a financial obstacle, according to a news story that year.

Fisk completed restoration of the building about two years ago and now uses it for programs to help international students, university officials said.

Richard Henry Boyd's larger 2 1/2-story home at 1602 Heiman St. did not fare as well. By the early 1970s, like much of that part of north Nashville, the brick house with this round tower was cut off from easy access by interstate construction-in this case, just across the street.

In the 1960s and 1970s it was sometimes vacant, other times occupied by various individuals and two successive daycare centers until 1982, when the city directory did not list the address at all.

In the years since its demolition, a row of modern residences has been built on the site, a block away from St. Vincent De Paul School. A cut stone wall across the street from where it had been still hints at the area's lost grandeur.

But Nashville's Boyd family is far from gone. Citizens Bank continues today, with one of its offices at 1917 Heiman St. Opened by Richard Henry Boyd and others in 1904 as One Cent Savings Bank, it has been described in recent years as one of the country's two oldest African-American-founded banks still in operation.

Also, T.B. Boyd III has continued since 1979 to head the publishing company founded by his great-grandfather. It was formerly governed by his father in 1959-79 and his great-uncle, Henry A. Boyd, in 1922-1959.

George Zepp writes about the people, places and things that make Nashville unique. SOURCES: Newspaper archives; "A Black Man's Dream," Bobby L. Lovett, 1993; Tennessee Encyclopedia of History and Culture, 1998; Handbook of Texas Online; "Nashville 1900 to 1910," William Waller, 1972; Metro Historical Commission; Metro Archives.

Used by permission of the Tennessean.

APPENDIX B

Significant Historical Events for the National Baptist Publishing Board/ R.H. Boyd Publishing Corporation

1843	Dick Gray (Richard H. Boyd) is born a slave in Mississippi
1848	Formation of the American Baptist Missionary Convention (founded, 1840), NY
1858	Slave Dick Gray moves to Texas
1863	President Abraham Lincoln's Emancipation Proclamation goes into effect, January
1865	Emancipation of the slaves by the Thirteenth Amendment, December 18
1866	Civil Rights Bill gives citizenship protection to the freedmen
1866	Consolidated American Baptist Missionary Convention formed, Richmond, Va.
1868	States ratify the Fourteenth Amendment to the Constitution—citizenship, equal protection of the laws and due process of the laws for persons born in the U.S.
1868	Dick Gray marries Laura Thomas, who dies eleven months later
1869	Dick Gray changes name to R.H. Boyd and professes religion and the ministry
1870	States ratify the 15th Amendment to the Constitution—voting and political rights
1871	R.H. Boyd marries Harriet A. Moore
1874	R.H. Boyd serves as Baptist district moderator in Texas
1875	Civil Rights Act—equal public accommodations regardless of color and race
1879	R.H. Boyd becomes moderator of Central Baptist Association in Texas
1880	Baptist Foreign Missionary Convention formed
1882	R.H. Boyd attends Bishop College, Marshall, Texas
1883	Supreme Court nullifies the Civil Rights Act of 1875
1886	American National Baptist Convention formed
1891	R.H. Boyd becomes pastor of Mt. Zion Baptist Church, San Antonio

1891	Southern Baptists form their own Sunday School Publishing Board
1892	Negro Baptists form the Baptist Educational Convention
1894	Boyd and others form Missionary Baptist General Convention of Texas
1895	R.H. Boyd and others in Texas form church book depository independent of the ABPS
1895	National Baptist Convention, USA, formed, Atlanta, September 28
1896	National Baptist Publishing Board formed, Nashville, November
1898	National Baptist Publishing Board officially chartered, Tennessee
1899	National Baptist Publishing Board publishes books
1904	One Cent Savings and Trust Co. Bank formed by R.H. Boyd and others, Nashville
1905	R.H. Boyd and NBPB officers conceive National Baptist Sunday School Congress
1906	First National Baptist Sunday School Congress held, Nashville
1907	NBPB opens new chapel in company's headquarters
1908	W.J. Tobias introduces Congress theme song, "Hail the Baptist Congress"
1909	R.H. Boyd announces building of a church and missionary in Panama
1910	NBPB revenues reach $200,000
1911	H.A. Boyd a leader among founders of Tennessee A&I State Normal School
1914	Boy Cadets and Church Drill Teams formed
1915	National Missionary Baptist Convention formed, Chicago
1917	Publishing Board supports nation's World War I efforts
1918	R.H. Boyd and NBCA open National Baptist Theological and Training Seminary
1922	R.H. Boyd dies, August 23, and is succeeded by son, Henry Allen Boyd
1924	Lott Carey Missionary Baptist Convention and NBPB form cooperative agreement
1944	NBPB and Sunday School Congress support nation's World War II efforts
1944	Citizens Bank (formerly One Cent Savings Bank) reaches $1 million, November
1950	NBPB doing more than $500,000 annually in business
1959	H.A. Boyd dies, May 28, and is succeeded by nephew, T.B. Boyd, Jr.
1963	NBPB assets reach $1 million

1975	NBPB builds new plant and headquarters on Centennial Boulevard
1979	T.B. Boyd, Jr. dies, April 1, and is succeeded by son, T.B. Boyd III
1979	Mini-Congress formed
1987	Renamed National Baptist Sunday Church School and Baptist Training Union Congress
1996	NBPB celebrates 100 years
1997	NBPB revenues exceed $10,000,000
2000	R.H. Boyd Publishing Corporation formed, January
2003	T.B. Boyd III named among "Most Influential African-American Leaders"
2005	The four major Black Baptist Conventions hold Joint Winter Board Meeting in Nashville, Tennessee
2006	One Hundredth Anniversary of the National Baptist Sunday School and Baptist Training Union Congress (Held at the Gaylord Opryland Resort Hotel and Convention Center, Nashville, TN, June 11-16)

APPENDIX C

Schedule of Cities Visited by the National Baptist Congress, 1906-2006

1906	Nashville	1947	Detroit
1907	New Orleans	1948	Kansas City, Missouri
1908	Jacksonville, Florida	1949	Dallas
1909	Nashville	1950	Chicago
1910	Atlanta	1951	San Francisco
1911	Meridian, Mississippi	1952	Houston
1912	Birmingham	1953	San Antonio
1913	Muskogee, Oklahoma	1954	Kansas City
1914	Beaumont	1955	Kansas City
1915	Birmingham	1956	Houston
1916	Vicksburg, Mississippi	1957	Cleveland, Ohio
1917	Nashville	1958	Fort Worth
1918	Alexandria, Louisiana	1959	Denver
1919	Bessemer, Alabama	1960	Chicago
1920	Springfield, Illinois	1961	Portland, Oregon
1921	Denver, Colorado	1962	Houston
1922	USA	1963	Kansas City
1923	USA	1964	Chicago
1924	USA	1965	Oakland, California
1925	USA	1966	New Orleans
1926	Columbia, S. Carolina	1967	Cincinnati
1927	Birmingham	1968	USA
1928	Louisville	1969	Chicago
1929	Cleveland, Ohio	1970	Kansas City
1930	Chicago	1971	Jackson
1931	Denver, Colorado	1972	Detroit
1932	Jacksonville, Florida	1973	Indianapolis
1933	Shreveport, Louisiana	1974	Ft. Worth
1934	Norfolk, Virginia	1975	Wichita
1935	Houston	1976	Kansas City
1936	New Orleans	1977	San Diego
1937	Cincinnati	1978	USA
1938	Kansas City, Missouri	1979	Chicago
1939	Indianapolis	1980	Dallas
1940	San Antonio	1981	Cleveland
1941	Chicago	1982	St. Louis
1942	Oklahoma City	1983	Chicago
1943	Dallas	1984	Orlando
1944	Houston	1985	Denver
1945	Fort Worth	1986	New Orleans
1946	Chicago	1987	Dallas

1988	Nashville	1998	Cincinnati
1989	Houston	1999	Houston
1990	New Orleans	2000	Fort Lauderdale
1991	Los Angeles	2001	Detroit
1992	Atlanta	2002	Phoenix
1993	Detroit	2003	St. Louis
1994	Columbus, Ohio	2004	Fort Worth
1995	Phoenix	2005	Charlotte
1996	Nashville	2006	Nashville
1997	Louisville		

Selected Bibliography

In addition to the sources cited in the Acknowledgements, the author used many of the NBPB publications, programs for the annual Sunday School Congress, and programs and minutes for black Baptist Conventions, as well as the following. The author gives due credit to all the authors and others whose books, articles, information, and studies have aided in completing this book.

Annuals of the Northern Baptist Convention. Nashville: SBC Historical Commission.

Annuals of the Northern Baptist Convention. Philadelphia: American Baptist Publication Society, 1910-10, available at the Nashville: SBC Historical Commission.

Annual Sessions of the National Baptist Convention, 1896-1915; Official Programs of the NBC. Nashville: National Baptist Publishing Board.

Bacote, Samuel W., ed. *Who's Who Among the Colored Baptists of the United States.* New York: Arno Press, 1913, 1980.

Baker, Robert A. The *Southern Baptist Convention and Its People, 1607-1972.* Nashville: Broadman Press, 1974.

Bass, Alwys. *Black Texans: A History of Negroes in Texas, 1529-1971.* Austin: University of Texas Press, 1973.

Brackney, William H. *The Baptists.* Westport, CT: Greenwood Press, 1988.

Brawley, Benjamin. *A Social History of the American Negro.* NY: New Publishers, 1913.

Boyd, R.H. *Story of the National Baptist Publishing Board.* Nashville: National Baptist Publishing Board, 1915.

Campbell, Randolph B. *An Empire of Slavery: The Peculiar Institution in Texas, 1821-1865.* Baton Rouge: Louisiana State University Press, 1869.

Caruthers, Sammie S. "A History of the Two Outstanding Negro Publishing Houses of the Nation Located in Nashville, Tennessee." M.S. thesis, Tennessee A. & I. State College, 1944.

Doyle, Don E. *Nashville Since the 1920s*. Knoxville: University of Tennessee Press, 1985.

Elkins, Larry. "Richard Henry Boyd: A Portrait, 1843-1922." M.S. thesis, Tennessee State University, 1972.

Fisher, Miles M. "Lott Carey, the Colonizing Missionary." *Journal of Negro History*, 7 (1922): 1-15.

Fitts, Leroy. *Lott Carey: First Black Missionary to Africa*. Valley Forge: PA: Judson Press, 1979.

Fuller, Thomas O. *History of the Negro Baptists in Tennessee*. Memphis: T.O. Fuller, 1936.

Harlan, Louis C. *The Booker T. Washington Papers, 1903-1904*. Urbana: University of Illinois Press, 1977.

Hiscox, Edward R. *The New Directory for Baptist Churches*. Philadelphia: American Baptist Publication Society, 1994.

Journals of the American National Baptist Convention. Microfilm is available at the SBC, Historical Commission, Nashville.

Journals of the National Baptist Convention of America (Unincorporated), SBC, Historical Commission, Nashville, and at the NBPB.

Joyce, Donald F. *Gatekeepers of Black Culture: Black Owned Book Publishing in the United States, 1817-1981*. West Port, CT: Greenwood Press, 1983.

Lack, Paul D. "Slavery and the Texas Revolution." *Southwestern Quarterly*, 89 (1985): 181-202.

Lovett, Bobby L. *The African-American History of Nashville, Tennessee, 1780-1930: Elites and Dilemmas*. Fayetteville: University of Arkansas Press, 1999.

Lovett, Bobby L. *A Black Man's Dream: The First One Hundred Years, the Story of R.H. Boyd and the National Baptist Publishing Board*. Nashville: Mega Corp., 1993.

Morris, Elias C. *Sermons, Addresses, Reminiscences, and Important Correspondence*. Nashville: NBPB, 1901.

Nashville Globe, 1906-1960.

National Baptist Union-Review, 1905-Present. Nashville, NBPB.

National Baptist Publishing Board's library and archives contain letters, documents, reports, photographs, and newspapers (laminated originals).

National Baptist Voice. Nashville: Sunday School Publishing Board, 1916-?

Pius, Nathaniel H. *An Outline of Baptist History.* Nashville: National Baptist Publishing Board, 1911.

Powell, Ruth M. *Ventures in Education with Black Baptists in Tennessee.* New York: Carlton Press, Inc., 1979.

Reports of the Annual Meeting of the Consolidated American Baptist Missionary Convention, available at the SBC Historical Commission, Nashville.

Rowland, Dunbar, ed. *Encyclopedia of Mississippi History,* 2 vols. Madison: University of Wisconsin Press, 1907.

Schweninger, *Black Property Owners in the South, 1790-1915.* Urbana, IL: University of Illinois Press, 1990.

Silverthorne, Elizabeth. *Plantation Life in Texas.* College Station: University of Texas Press, 1986.

Smith, R.L. and O.D. Pelt, *The Story of the National Baptists.* New York: Vantage Press, 1960.

Torbet, Robert G. *A History of the Baptists.* Philadelphia: Judson Press, 1950.

Tucker, David M. *Black Pastors and Leaders: Memphis, 1919-1972.* Memphis, TN: Memphis State University Press, 1975.

Wardin, Albert W., Jr. *Tennessee Baptists: A Comprehensive History, 1779-1999.* Brentwood, TN: Tennessee Baptist Convention, 1999.

Washington, James M. *Frustrated Fellowship: The Black Baptist Quest for Social Power.* Macon, GA: Mercer University Press, 1986.

Woodson, Carter G. *The History of the Negro Church.* Washington, D.C.: Associated University Publishers, 1945.

Zepp, George. *Mansions Symbolized Success of Ex-slave Descendants.* The Tennessean, 20 September 2006.

INDEX ━━━━━━━━━━━━━━━━━━━

A

Abner, E.M., 37
Abner, D., Jr., 11
Abner, R., 9
Adams, John H., 137, 178
Adkins, E.W., 13
Alabama A. & M., 8
Allen, M.C., 110
AME Sunday School Union, 7
Alexander, H.A., 132
American Baptist Home Mission
   Society, xii, xviii, 7, 10, 11, 16, 18,
   20, 43, 56
American Baptist Publication Society,
   xii, 11, 12, 18, 19, 20, 27, 37, 55,
   203, 205
American Baptist Missionary
   Convention, 8, 14, 15, 16, 58, 162,
   178, 197, 205
American Baptist Theological
   Seminary, 128
American National Baptist
   Convention, 14, 17, 18, 21, 32, 158,
   170
Antioch Missionary Baptist Church,
   97, 127, 141
Atlanta Baptist College, 56

B

Baker, W.R., 66
Ball, W.B., 21
Baptist Educational Convention, 18,
   20, 21, 178
Baptist Foreign Mission Convention,
   16-18, 21, 39, 86, 178
Baptist Herald, 36
Baptist Vanguard, 30
Battle, Joseph O., 40
Beale Street Baptist Church, 90, 92, 93
Beckham, William, 21, 42, 43, 55, 57
Bell, T.P., 12-14
Benton, Hezekiah, 138
Binkley, W.A., 16

Bishop College, 7, 10, 44, 149
Black, Bernard, 160-161
Bobo, Ronald, 160-161
Bone, R.A., 54
Booth, C.O., 37
Borden, E.H., 96
Boscobel College, 78, 79
Bowie, A. Charles, 138, 142-143, 159
Bowman, A.L., 132
Boy Cadets, xviii, 63-65, 88, 97
Boyd, Henry Allen, xi, xviii, 48-50, 63,
   64, 77, 78, Chapter 5, 110, 133,
   147-148, 195
Boyd, Mable (Landrum), 111, 117, 130,
   159
Boyd, R.H., Chapters 1-4; Chapters 7-
   8, 194 Harriett 32, xiii, xiv, xvii,
   xviii, xix, xx
Boyd, R.H., Memorial Commission,
   68, 95
Boyd, T.B. III, Chapters 7-8; Yvette
   (Duke), xii, xiii, xix, 131-133, 159,
   164, 170, 190, 191
Boyd, T.B., Jr., Chapter 5-6, xiii, xix,
   115
Boyd, T.B., Jr., Scholarship , 130, 135
Bradford, Georgia (Boyd), 85, 99
Branch, E.H., 90, 94, 102
Brawley, E.M., 17, 37
Brooks, Darrell, 141
Brooks, Walter H., 37
Brown, J.H., 48
Brown, J.T., 37, 53
Butts, Calvin, 160

C

California MB State Convention, 143
Campbell, I.S., 8
Campbell, L.L., 21, 36, 65
Cansler, Charles, 34
Cansler, W.L., 32, 67
Carter, E.R., 29, 32, 37, 88
Chambers, L.V., 63

Chautauqua Movement, 13
Church of God in Christ, 46, 137, 177
Church, Robert R. 93
Churchwell, Robert, 146, 147
Citizens Bank, ii, xviii, 67, 83, 86, 87,
    90, 93, 96, 106, 107, 129, 130, 145,
    146, 148, 150, 182, 187, 195, 198
Clark, Charles H., iii, xi, 31, 32, 39, 48,
    50, 52, 60, 65, 88
Cohron, J.L., 37
Cole, Lucy, 37
Coleman, Quaford C., 144
Colored YMCA, 60, 63, 67, 80, 86, 89,
    113
Colley, William W., 16
Consolidated AB Missionary
    Convention, 8, 15, 16, 178, 197, 205
Cook, M.V., 37
Corbett, Maurice, 53
Crawford, W.H., 63, 64
Credit, W.A., 37
Crump, Edward H., 90, 92, 93, 94, 95

D
Daniel, W.N., v, 97, 111, 116, 127, 128,
    136, 137, 153, 163
Davis, F. Benjamin, v, 97, 128, 135, 141,
    159, 163, 167
Davis, Nehemiah, v, 153, 155, 159, 163
Davis, Ruth L., 133
DeBaptiste, Georgia A., 58, 59
DeBaptiste, Richard, 15, 37
Dexter Avenue Baptist Church, 38
Dickson, Indiana (Annie), 48, 57
Drill Teams, see Boy Cadets
DuBois, William E.B., xiv, 16, 19, 22,
    189

E
East Mt. Zion Baptist Church, 138, 142
Eason, J.H., 53
Ebenezer Baptist Church, iv, 60, 87, 94,
    95, 100, 150
Ellington, W.S., 49, 57
Ensley, Deborah Scott, 145, 146
Evergreen Baptist Church, 113
Ewing, T.G., 34-36

F
Fielder, J.C., 65
Fireside School, xviii, 41, 43, 55
First Colored Baptist Church, 14, 15,
    17, 18, 31, 33, 49, 57, 112, 115
First Shiloh Baptist Church, 113
Fisk University, xii, xiv, 63, 67, 85, 89,
    107, 111, 144, 146, 156, 166, 195
Fisher, E.J., 39
Florida Progressive Baptist
    Convention, 60
Frank, J.H., 58
Friendship Baptist Church, 88, 116, 141
Frost, James M., xii, 12, 31, 32, 34, 38,
    42, 54, 58
Full Gospel, 176, 179, 180

G
Gaines, G.W.D., 29, 30, 32, 38, 39
General Baptist SS Congress of
    Alabama, 64
General Baptist Missionary Western
    States and Territories Association,
    17
Geter, J., 29, 30, 32
Gholson, R.H., 132
Gilbert, Meredith W., 18
Girls Doll Clubs, xviii
Globe Publishing Company, 77
Great Migration, xix, 93, 97
Greater New Mt. Moriah Baptist
    Church, 140
Greater St. James Baptist Church, 97
Greater Salem Baptist Church, 111
Greater Temple of God MB Church,
    143
Graham, W.F., 37
Gray, Dick, 3-7, 197
Greenwood Cemetery, 46, 67, 89, 98
Greenwood Giants Baseball Team, 58
Greenwood Park, 58, 63, 86, 89
Griggs, S.E., 9, 54
Groves, D., 160
Guadalupe College, 8, 37, 57, 113
Guess, Francis, 164

H

Hail the Baptist Congress, 50, 51, 62, 198
Harding, J.L., 65
Harris, Solomon P., 36, 37, 38
Hart, Dock A., 40, 77
Hausey, W.E., 106, 133
Hemphill, W.D., 19, 21
Hearne College, 57
Herald Publishing Co., 18
Highlander Folk School, 109
Hill, E.V., 141, 144
Hobson, Lula I, 32, 33
Holiness Church, 30
Holley, Jim, v, 139, 140, 160, 168
Hooks, Benjamin, 136, 139, 155, 170
Hope magazine, xviii, 41, 96
Hopewell Baptist Church, 7
Huffman, T., 31
Hurse, J.W., 88
Hurt, Allen D., 33, 39, 53

I

International Sunday School Lesson, 60, 61
Isaac, E.W.D., 9-11, 28, 49, 67

J

Jackson, M.L., 159
Jim Crow, xviii, xix, 10, 11, 13, 19, 22, 23, 28, 48, 49, 64, 77, 80, 81, 91, 176, 185, 186
Johnson, H.B.P., 62, 94
Johnson, W. Bishop, 18
Jones, E.P., 58, 65, 67
Jones, S.S., 88
Jordan, I.J., 35
Jordan, Lewis G., xi, 32, 53

K

Kayne Avenue Baptist Church, 35
Kellar, Marcel, 115, 160
Kennedy, M.C., 37
King, Martin Luther, Jr., 92, 109, 111, 112, 114, 121, 129, 179

L

Lake Providence Baptist Church, 60, 113
LeMoyne College, 57
Lawrence, Emmanuel M., 35; Lillie, 35
Lawson, James M., Jr., 112, 147
Leland University, 57
Liberty Baptist Church, 59
Lincoln, Abraham, 5, 65, 197
Lincoln Baptist District Association, 8
Lincoln Douglass Voters League, 85, 86
Little Rock MB Church, 139, 140, 160
Lockridge, S.M., v, 133, 136, 153
Long, Eddie, 138, 140
Long, George A., 90-93
Lott Carey Convention, 21, 39, 86, 163, 174, 198
Love, E.K., 28

M

Matthews, Articia, 136
McGirt's magazine, 49
McKinney, Julia (Singleton), 35
Meharry Medical College,iii, 26, 85, 89, 129, 133, 143, 166
Merry, Nelson G., 14, 15, 17
Methodist Publishing House, 35
Metropolitan Baptist Church, 141, 142
Missionary Baptist General Convention, 11, 18, 27-29, 59, 149, 198
Moore, Harriett Albertine (see also R.H. Boyd) 7, 29, 197
Moore, Joanna, 41
Moore, J.M., 29, 31
Morehouse College, 7, 56, 141
Morehouse, Henry L., 17, 44, 56
Morris, Elias C., iii, 17, 20, 27-29, 34, 36, 39, 40, 41, 43, 53, 55, 56, 67, 74, 204
Mt. Calvary Missionary Baptist Church, 142, 158
Mt. Moriah Baptist Church, 144
Mt. Olive Baptist Church, iii, 17, 31, 32, 34, 48, 53, 60, 74, 95, 98, 115,

116, 122, 151, 160, 166
Mt. Tabor Baptist Church, 93
Mt. Zion Baptist Church, 9, 10, 11, 63, 138, 141, 142, 197

N
Napier, J.C., iv, xiv, 79, 80, 82, 146
Nashville Christian Leadership Council, 112
National Bankers' Association, 145
National Baptist Chorus, 59
National Baptist Church Furniture Co., xvii
National Baptist Congress Band, 63-65, 84
National Baptist Convention, Inc., Chapters 2, 3, xi, 112, 176, 179, 180
National Baptist Convention of America and NMBCA, xii, 58-60, 62, 64, 78, 81, 86, 88, 89, 109, 125, 133, 134, 137, 147, 148, 179, 180, 186, 204
National Baptist Magazine, 18
National Baptist Publishing Board, Chapters 1-7
National Baptist Sunday School Congress, Chapters 1-8
National Baptist Theological Seminary and Training School, 78, 88, 198
National Baptist Union-Review, Chapters 3-8
National Baptist Young People's Union, 20
National Negro Business League, xvii, 79, 146
New Bethel Baptist Church, 97, 116, 163
New Birth Baptist Church, 138
New Hope Baptist Church, 10, 149
New Tower MB Church, 129
New Year's Day Banquet, NBPB, 36, 86
Noble, B.W., 143, 159
Northeast Baptist Miss. Convention, 16
Northwestern and Southern Baptist

Convention, 15

O
One Cent Savings Bank (See also Citizens Bank), iv, xvii, 75, 79, 80, 82, 196, 198

P
Panama, iii, 54, 55, 60, 71, 90, 95, 97, 198
Parrish, Charles H., 28, 37
People's Defender, 88
People's MB Church, 129
Perry, Rufus, 9, 16
Pickens, William 94
Pitt, J.W., 88
Pius, Nathaniel H., 50, 51, 56, 57, 62, 205
Pleasant Green Baptist Church, 32, 63
Pounds, Roderick C., 141
Prince, G.L., iv, 95, 96, 98, 104, 109
Progressive National Baptist Convention, 112, 176, 179, 180, 186

R
Randal, Lena, 33, 38
Randolph, A. Philip, 92
Refuge Missionary Baptist Church, 141
R.H. Boyd Publishing Co., Chapter 8, v, vii, xiii, xiv, xix, 152, 174, 176, 177, 179, 180, 187, 188, 190, 197, 199
Rhinehart, J.J., 7
Ridley, John R., 60
Robinson, J.P., iii, 30, 39, 40, 52, 65, 88
Roger Williams University, 7, 10, 20, 27, 32, 35, 55
Roseborough, William, 53, 94
Rowland, A.J., 34, 55; see ABPS

S
St. John Institutional Church, 133
St. Stephen Baptist Church, 116
Satcher, David, 133
Sardis MB Church, 129
Saul, Ruth, 136
Seastrong, Betty, 141
Searcy, T.J., 31
Shaw, William, 160, 186

Sherwood, W.H., 41
Silver Bluff Baptist Church, xii, 16, 162
Simmons, William J., 16
Simpson, S.H, 113
Singleton, J.B., 35, 36
Smith, C.S., 31
Smith, Henry K., 143
Smith, Kelly Miller, 112, 131
Snead, Willie T., 143, 149, 150
South Phoenix Baptist Church, 160
South Union Baptist Church, 14
Southern Baptist Convention, xii, xiii,
    xviii, 11, 12, 14, 15, 18, 19, 21, 27,
    36, 37 42, 57, 58, 59, 175, 176, 179,
    203
Southern Christian Leadership
    Conference, 112, 138
Stones River MB District Association,
    32, 60, 113
Summer Street Baptist Church, 32, 34
Supreme Life Insurance Co., 85

T
Taylor, G.C., ix, 160, 166, 171
Taylor, G.B., 60, 65
Taylor, Preston, 67, 77, 80
Temple, R.J., 28
Tennessee Baptist Missionary and
    Educational Convention, 176
Tennessee State University, xii, 78, 98,
    111, 115, 125, 131, 139, 145-147,
    150, 164, 166, 195, 204
Texas Negro Baptist Convention, 8, 9,
    11, 13, 27, 28
Thomas, James, 150
Thomas, Laura (Gray), 7, 197
Thorburne, R.H., iii, 71, 95
Tobias, T.W., 50, 51, 62, 94, 198
Trower, John S., 45
Turner, G. Thomas, 135, 159
Turner, J.H., 94

U
Union Baptist Church, 98, 132
Union Transportation Company, 77
V

Vann, Michael, 17, 31, 32, 38
Vass, S.N., iii, 28, 32, 38, 46, 72
Virginia Union Seminary, 7, 79

W
Wade, Melvin V., Sr., 144, 161, 162, 163,
    186
Wardin, A.W., 16, 176, 205
Washington, Booker T., 9, 19, 20, 23,
    79, 146, 189, 204
Washington, Donald, 141
Waters, W., 14
West Side Missionary Baptist Church,
    160, 161
West Union Baptist Church, 85
White, R.L., 138
Williams, H.H., 11
Williams, O.B., 142
Wilson, Sadie B., iv, 89, 105
Wilson, Woodrow, 64
Winfrey, Oprah, 147
Wood, W.H., 64
Woods, Bob, 34
Woodson, Carter G., xiii, 51, 86, 205
Wright, S.M., iii, 134, 148, 149, 154
Wyatt, Bryant C., 142

Z
Zion Baptist Church, 112

Printed in the United States
66166LVS00004B/1-126

9 781890 436278